The Five Fold Ministry: Gifts to the Church

Chris A. Legebow

DEDICATION

I thank God for giving me special favour permitting me to receive directly
from Apostles, Prophets, Evangelists, Pastors and Teachers.
I thank God for Christian Media that broadcasts the five-fold ministry
preaching and teaching.

CONTENTS

ACKNOWLEDGMENTS

All scripture taken from Bible Gateway.com
King James Version
Modern English Version
New International Version

1 INTRODUCTION

Ephesians 4: 11 He gave some to be apostles, prophets, evangelists, pastors, and teachers, 12 for the equipping of the saints, for the work of service, and for the building up of the body of Christ, 13 until we all come into the unity of the faith and of the knowledge of the Son of God, into a complete man, to the measure of the stature of the fullness of Christ,

Truly Jesus rose triumph and over death, hell and the grave. When he ascended into heaven visibly with more than 500 witnesses, He promised to send the Holy Spirit. He instructed his disciples to go to Jerusalem and to wait for the gift of the Holy Spirit. I do not believe the disciples knew what they were waiting for but 120 of them, men and women, obeyed.

Acts 2: 2 When the day of Pentecost had come, they were all together in one place. 2 Suddenly a sound like a mighty rushing wind came from heaven, and it filled the whole house where they were sitting. 3 There appeared to them tongues as of fire, being distributed and resting on each of them, 4 and they were all filled with the Holy Spirit and began to speak in other tongues, as the Spirit enabled them to speak.

The disciples were baptized with the Holy Spirit and the gifts of the Holy Spirit were released in the earth in the Church. The disciples had been empowered by the Holy Spirit, so strongly it compelled them to go into the streets below as they continued praising God and giving glory to God. As a direct result, over 2, 000 people received Jesus as Saviour and were water baptized and filled with the Holy Spirit. Because of the presence of the Holy Spirit in the earth, the Church multiplied and continues to multiply. There are millions of Christians throughout the earth because of Jesus' promise to send the Holy Spirit.

The Holy Spirit is not a thing. He is a person, part of the Trinity. The Holy Spirit is God's Holy presence living on the inside of those who believe in Jesus Christ. As soon as a person receives Jesus Christ as Saviour, the person's spirit is born again or renewed. The old sin nature dies and a new spiritual life in Christ begins. Christianity is not just a religion of people

1

who believe in Jesus; Christianity is a people who have received the living God dwelling on the inside of them. Christians carry the Holy Spirit with them wherever they go. God lives in us. The Baptism of the Holy Spirit is an experience we are promised.

Acts 2: 38 Peter said to them, "Repent and be baptized, every one of you, in the name of Jesus Christ for the forgiveness of sins, and you shall receive the gift of the Holy Spirit. 39 For the promise is to you, and to your children, and to all who are far away, as many as the Lord our God will call."

The gift of the Holy Spirit is God living on the inside of a believer. To be baptized in the Holy Spirit, the person is immersed in the Holy Spirit by Jesus Christ just as a person baptizes a believer in water. They are immersed. As the Holy Spirit is a person, He has various expressions that will transform us from glory to glory in Christ likeness (2 Corinthians 3: 18). What is included is Spiritual fruit or godly character (Galatians 5: 22- 23) and Spiritual gifts or manifestations of the Holy Spirit through a believer (1 Corinthians 12: 7-11). I have discussed the gifts of the Holy Spirit in much detail in my book on Spiritual Gifts: knowing them and Using them.

Often neglected in studies of Spiritual gifts is the Ministry gifts. God not only gave manifestations gifts, and motivational gifts but also ministry gifts. Ministry gifts are a calling for life's service – usually your career path is formed by it. The study of this book is to give some insight to the ministry gifts and the characteristics of each gift as well as some important information about them.

 I have had the privilege to receive much excellent preaching and teaching throughout my life. I've also had the freedom to receive Christian Media so excellent that it has enriched my life beyond what words explain. I have had the special honour of having been taught by people from all of the five-fold ministry gifts. It is from this direct experience with the five-fold ministry that I bring the teaching on the apostles, Prophets, Evangelists, pastors and Teachers. I believe this book can encourage you should you simply want to know more about the ministry gifts or should you feel a tugging at your heart for ministry.

2 APOSTLES

The Five-fold Ministry Gifts: Apostles

Jesus resurrection from the dead and ascension gives believers hope pf eternal life. Also, Jesus sent the Holy Spirit to come live within us. There are different types of giftings that are a result of the Holy Spirit. There are the manifestation gifts 1Corinthians 12: 7-13: gift of faith, gift of working of miracle, gifts of healing, gift of word of wisdom, gift of word of knowledge, gift of discerning of spirits, gift of tongues and interpretation of tongues, gift of prophecy. The motivational gifts (Romans 12: 6-8) include teaching, serving, giving, exhorting, mercy, leading. In my book on Spiritual gifts; knowing them and using them I discuss these gifts in much detail. Also, there are ministry gifts: apostle, prophet, evangelist, pastor and teacher. This book will focus on the aspects of those who feel called to ministry as zeal prompting them to live their lives for God in ministry.

Ephesians 4: 7 But grace was given to each one of us according to the measure of the gift of Christ. 8 Therefore He says:
"When He ascended on high,
  He led captivity captive,
  and gave gifts to men."[a]

Ephesians 4: 11 He gave some to be apostles, prophets, evangelists, pastors, and teachers, 12 for the equipping of the saints, for the work of service, and for the building up of the body of Christ, 13 until we all come into the unity of the faith and of the knowledge of the Son of God, into a complete man, to the measure of the stature of the fullness of Christ,

Ministers

Everyone in the body of Christ has a ministry of some type but not all explore a career choice of ministering in a church or Christian organization. The person who feels a strong compulsion to minister will sometimes be overwhelmed with the passion to do it. This can occur at any part of a person's life. Youth called to ministry included Oral Roberts, Lester Summerall and Kenneth Hagin. Others, called into ministry could already be in a career and successful and could make a good living but they feel a strong desire to serve God by going into ministry full time. An example would be Smith Wigglesworth who was a successful plumber and John G. Lake who was a successful businessman. Both became healing evangelists who reached thousands of people.

The Day of Pentecost released the baptism of the Holy Spirit on the disciples who were praying and expecting Jesus to send the Holy Spirit as was promised. They were overwhelmed with the Spirit and spoke in tongues. The feeling was so strong, it compelled them to go into the streets preaching and praising God in tongues (Acts 2). The disciples of Jesus became known as the Apostles of Jesus. Jesus had chosen 12 of them. But that was not the end of the gifting.

Several years later on the road to Damascus, Saul of Tarsus a Pharisee who fought against Christians encountered the LORD Jesus Christ and was transformed. Jesus revealed Himself sovereignly to Saul and called him to preach the gospel. He became known as Apostle Paul who ministered mostly to the Gentiles. He was one of the main missionaries who brought the gospel throughout the East and also Europe. Afterwards, others were appointed the title of Apostle which means sent ones.

Some denominational churches have Bishops who are the equivalent of Apostles. They often oversee several churches or a territory. Some denominational churches do not use the term bishop or Apostle but they have regional superintendents who are functioning as Apostles. In the 1980's in the Church of North America, arose a strong movement upon the Prophets of God. Towards the end of the 1980's and into 1990's there has been the release of many Apostles. Apostles often care for several churches. They usually start a church or missionary base and train others to oversee them. Usually, they travel from place to place.

It is my desire that you should come to know something about these ministry gifts so that you would thank God for the people God places in your life and be able to recognize their giftings and get the most you can from them. Also, perhaps some of you may feel a strong calling for ministry. It's possible something I share might encourage you and lead you to others who can give you much more information about the gifts. If you know you have these ministry giftings it is important to be aligned with people who believe the same as you, or who can encourage you in developing your gifts,

Apostles Train Others

Apostles are to "train up others" for the work of the ministry. Literally, they teach, equip, release and appoint other ministers in the Church. They build churches; they train up others. Their main focus is on training others and bringing people to know the giftings and calling of God on their lives so that the Body of Christ would be built up and strengthened. They are gifted leaders who usually flow in all of the ministry gifts or some measure and certainly flow in many manifestation and motivational gifts. The anointing on Apostles is undeniable – they are larger than life. The anointing is on them so strong, people give their lives to Christ, rededicate their lives to God and give their lives to ministry. The only way I can describe it is that a normal leader would be a flashlight or a strong beam light but Apostles are like stadium lights for a game. The atmosphere is lit up because of them.

Apostles carry a legacy of truths of Church history, church doctrines, the foundations and the future direction of the church often having been a part of revival services or living through revivals. They care about the teaching of the church and the foundation of Jesus Christ alone as the way of salvation. They desire to give us, the body of Christ, the best possible so that we can effectively be ministers of reconciliation or soul winners. All of the ministry gifts function to connect and impart into the body of Christ.

Jesus chose the 12 disciples, even though he knew that Judas would betray him. They travelled with Jesus, saw the miracles, heard the teachings; they were immersed in Jesus and the gospel of salvation. Jesus knew those men had to bring the truths he taught them throughout Israel, but also throughout all the earth. They had no airplanes and transportation was walking, riding a horse or a donkey, or travelling by ship. They had no television or radio, yet these simple men, most of them fishermen brought the truths of Christ all over the region and all over the earth.

Acts 1: 8 But you shall receive power when the Holy Spirit comes upon you. And you shall be My witnesses in Jerusalem, and in all Judea and Samaria, and to the ends of the earth."
The Multiplication of the Church

First there were 12. Later there were 70. At Jesus' ascension over 500 people gathered. 120 were baptized with the Holy Spirit speaking in other tongues on the day of Pentecost. On the day of Pentecost, the apostle Peter preached to over 2, 000 people who had gathered to worship God at Pentecost. They received Jesus as Saviour and were baptized in the Holy Spirit. The church did not grow in increments; it multiplied. Even though they were persecuted, they continued, some of them worshipping secretly and some of them living in the underground tunnels of Rome.

There are some churches that teach that an Apostle must see Jesus. That was true of the 12 Apostles. It was true of the Apostle Paul and it is certainly true of many others. I don't know if it is true of every apostle who ever lived. It is usually one of the attributes discussed acknowledging an Apostle. The people will have had personal experiences speaking with God and hearing from God directly. Often they are given instructions about their future and what they are to do.

Apostles are sent to bring the good news of the gospel. The life, death, burial, resurrection and ascension of Jesus are the main truths. The living Christ is truly their message as often there are manifestations of the giftings of the Spirit in their meetings. They start missionary organizations, plant churches, start Christian organizations and see their ministry mostly as global. Some are appointed to a region or territory.

The early apostles started no denomination. They were followers of Jesus – sometimes known as people of the way. It wasn't until the Apostle Paul was at Antioch that the Church because known as Christians or followers of Jesus Christ. Some of the modern day Apostles I know of are not necessarily attached to a denomination. It is not simply a title. The signs of an Apostle are upon them and they function in these strong giftings. There are some denominations who do not believe apostles exist today. I believe they have never seen or heard an apostle preach or teach or they would feel differently.

There are people who have the title Apostle so and so but they do not really have the unction. I am talking about the unction of the Holy Spirit that compels an apostle to teach and preach Christ and train up others to do the same. I have been privileged to sit in the anointing of several Apostles and because of Christian Broadcasting I have been able to glean much from those who are televised. The most prominent word I would say about all of them is they are passionate, zealous for God and for the Church Universal as well as local congregations. The fruit of an Apostle includes, salvation, healing, deliverance, the Baptism of the Holy Spirit, the working of miracles. Often, they connect Christians throughout their nation and internationally with other Christian congregations through missions and hosting speakers from those places. Often, they bring in other five-fold ministry gifts including other Apostles. What it does is bring excitement and expectancy to the services. People know that God will be present in the service. Should you get the opportunity to get teaching from an Apostle – go. It is worth it.

The truths they teach will seem so clear and real because of their zeal and their gift of communication. The manifestations of the spirit will be in the service and whether or not you are in the prayer line, you can receive a miracle. I would describe being in an Apostle's service as a boost to your faith. The gift of faith is usually so strong in those meetings, you are most certain to receive something that will transform your life. Also, the gift of working of miracles and gifts of healing are evident by people being healed or receiving a miracle. Literally, lame people receive strength in their legs can walk or run. Literally, blind eyes receive sight; the deaf can hear; those who were crippled are healed. Often people are released in their giftings such as prophecy or tongues or interpretation. I have witnessed people so excited by an Apostle's ministry gifts and the anointing that comes on the service so strong that people literally run.

They often operate in the prophetic realm. They may see visions or prophesy over the meeting in a way that brings a new life or a new opportunity for the people. People may receive revelations of ministry or giving. People will be energized, refreshed and strengthened.

Apostles can bring revival to a church. First of all, people who know of them will get excited and expecting and tell others. There becomes an opportunity for faith to be sparked. I have seen Apostles greeted with such cheering and clapping that I couldn't help but get excited myself. The demeanor is usually humble but with the boldness of Christ so that as they share the word of God, it is as though they are sharing from within themselves. They usually tell of miracles and healings and with simplicity preach healings and miracles.

They can command respect by their testimonies, as the signs of an Apostle are usually evident in their lives. I have been in services where collections were taken for the Apostle's ministry missionary trips and thousands of thousands were given without fund raising techniques; people gave large amounts because they knew the apostle would use it to bring the truths of Christ to people. People will give to them because the anointing of God is on them to do the works of God such as build and establish churches; build Bible colleges, establish missionary organizations that will directly help the people in their sphere of influence, including food, clothing, shelter etc.

The true Apostle is not trusting in people to finance his or her ministry. The true apostle knows God is the only source; he or she gives God all the glory. The people respond because they can see the fruit of a true apostle. They can be men or women. The gifts of the Church are for the body of Christ.

Galatians 3: 28 There is neither Jew nor Gentile, neither slave nor free, nor is there male and female, for you are all one in Christ Jesus.

Lester Sumerall

I saw a true Apostle: Lester Sumerall. If you have not read any of his books, I would highly recommend them. He founded Le Sea Ministries a missionary organization that would give food, clothing, shelter etc. as well as preach the Word of God to people throughout the earth. I had known of his preaching and watched him on TV. He was in his late 70's and he was training other ministers and they could hardly keep up with him because of his pace. He lived on the royalties from his teaching materials and all the money that was given to the missionary organization was directed to the missionary organization.

The Church was completely full; at least 2, 000 people were there. Lester Sumerall talked about what God had spoken to him directly. He was in Jerusalem Israel and God spoke to him that Jesus was coming soon and there were Christians who were in some countries such as countries in Africa where the people were Christians and they were praying for God to supply their daily bread but they were dying of starvation. God said it was because the Christians in other countries were not caring for the other members of the body of Christ in those other nations. God showed him that if a Christian would give up an extra fast food meal or a specialized dessert, there would be more than enough food to care for those Christians who were living in harsh conditions.

As he spoke, it was completely silent in the room. He shared how he was going to do anything he could to help those Christians in Africa. He shared how some of the governments persecuted Christians and were corrupt and so that is food was donated to the government, they often sold it on a black market and withheld food from the Christians. He saw that he needed to get the food to the people themselves and he would do it through the churches in those countries. The biggest expense was not the food and water but the cost of shipping.

He was so well respected by authorities and corporations because of his life of giving directly to the needs of others, that the US donated a huge bomber plane and they used it to fly food packages to people in remote areas. I'm not sure if it was the US navy or some other branch, donated a huge war ship. They completed tore out the guts of these war machines and turned them into transportation that brought hope and life to people. Kellogg phoned his organization and donated thousands of boxes of rice crispies. Other companies and corporations would also donate food and supplies they had a surplus of. He travelled extensively throughout most if not all of the continents.

At the end of his message, he reminded us that we are the body of Christ and we should care for other members of the body even though we may not see them on earth, the pastor of the church stood and pledged so many thousand dollars per month and also stated they would fast and pray for those Christians. The church was moved to give. I don't remember how many hundreds of thousands of dollars came in. He was humble. He was honest. His voice had authority and the proof of his ministry was his life long integrity as a minister, evangelist, pastor, Apostle.

Apostles must live a godly life

I saw an Apostle who had been well known especially for his interdenominational preaching and founding of churches. He was quite famous and preached travelling and training up others for many decades. His Church grew from hundreds to over 5,000. The building itself was so beautiful it was magnificent. There were stained glass windows and large comfortable cushioned pews. There was a huge property around the church and a restaurant and books store God had truly prospered them. The signs of excellence were in all the building materials and the staff. It had been a place of blessing for God's people and a place to bring people to be saved. Dramas, musicals and other outreaches into the community were parts of its outreach program.

He was known in his community because of their help as a food bank, and a work skills' training center. He appeared all over television and radio for decades. There was terrible scandal in his family; it included sexual immorality with the church members. It included things that dragged his name, and with it all true Christians, through a slander and media extravaganza. I had seen the writing about him but still chose to go to the church not knowing if the media was lying or if could be true.

The congregation had dwindled down to about 1, 000. The service was different because no people were welcome to greet the pastor. He was escorted into the service by deacons and out of the service by deacons. His words were scripture as he spoke; there was no fault in them. What I noticed is that his church that remained were his fans not his congregation. They esteemed him as a rock star or a sports hero. The demeanor was not humble or meek. My spirit was so grieved during the service that I knew I was witnessing what can happen should money or sex or pride enter a leader's heart. I believed that the reports of the immorality were true; later more evidence came through the media, including illegitimate children from adultery. My response is that truly someone who had potential to finish strong in his life had been captivated by the blessings that can come to an Apostle or minister of God.

I was not angry; I am grieved over the loss of someone who could have been written about in history books to glorify God with all of his life. The effect that such a devastating thing has on the sheep cannot be measured by earthly standards. Not only do the sheep scatter; they are wounded; the place that was to be a place of safety and comfort and care was used to abuse the sheep. I don't mention it to show the devil's victory; I state it to show that all people are human, all people must honour God as God; ministry must live to a pure standard of holiness. The results affect thousands of thousands of people when it is an Apostle.

Signs of an Apostle

True Apostles not only have signs and wonders but integrity of character and a life of sincere commitment and consecration to God. Miracles, signs and wonders are prevalent in their meetings but they are the evidences of what is within the spirit of the person. The Apostle Paul gives us a list of signs of an Apostle.

2 Corinthians 11: 23…I am more. I have worked much harder, been in prison more frequently, been flogged more severely, and been exposed to death again and again. 24 Five times I received from the Jews the forty lashes minus one. 25 Three times I was beaten with rods, once I was pelted with stones, three times I was shipwrecked, I spent a night and a day in the open sea, 26 I have been constantly on the move. I have been in danger from rivers, in danger from bandits, in danger from my fellow Jews, in danger from Gentiles; in danger in the city, in danger in the country, in danger at sea; and in danger from false believers. 27 I have labored and toiled and have often gone without sleep; I have known hunger and thirst and have often gone without food; I have been cold and naked. 28 Besides everything else, I face daily the pressure of my concern for all the churches. 29 Who is weak, and I do not feel weak? Who is led into sin, and I do not inwardly burn?

Although the Apostle Paul suffered, he let none of those things stop him from preaching and teaching Christ. He did not brag in his own strength but gave God the glory for seeing him through all of those situations. Notice the apostle Paul calls all of those trials as "external things' that were done to him. He also mentions his care for the churches as though it were equal to the first list. They passionately care for all the churches they minister in and they pray over congregations and ministry teams and are as a spiritual covering for them.

Not all people will rejoice in Apostles. They will be hated by those who hate Christ. There are many countries today where it is not possible for Christians to live freely. In those countries, the five-fold ministry usually become the martyrs of the Church. The apostles I have known of, from North America, have had their lives threatened as they prepared to preach in a crusade. Some literally faced a gunman or person who tried to kill them in the meeting. Miraculously, they lived to tell how they were spared. One apostle I know was with a ministry team in a car surrounded by a mob shaking and pounding on the windows with the mob of people trying to overturn the car, and it was by some miracle they were scattered. I have known of an apostle who was put into prison in China because he was a Christian Pastor.

All the guards they put around him kept getting saved. Even though they beat him, even though they treated him poorly, he kept preaching Christ to them and would not renounce his faith. Eventually, he was released from prison just as mysteriously as he was put in. He had made many converts. Upon return to his church, he had prayed for his church and hoped it would still flourish, he found that it had multiplied and believers had been strengthened because they had heard of his boldness in preaching Christ.

In North America, the Apostles usually face slander attacks and media scrutiny but also are usually respected and have the freedom to preach openly; people may believe they live cushioned lives. I do not diminish the Apostle who has not faced death threats because of being on assignment in North America rather than in a different part of the world. The same demons who conspire to kill Apostles in other nations, conspire to bad mouth the Apostles in our part of the world. Our response should be to pray for our leaders and to pray scriptures over their lives.

Personal conversations with Jesus

Usually, they have had some personal encounter earlier in their lives with Jesus that includes a divine healing or miracle. They can quote the words Jesus spoke to them. They are sometimes shown things of their lives, long before they happen. God gives them to us as His gift to us. Not all people understand the importance of these people to the Body of Christ. I thank God for each apostle I have received teaching from. I thank God for the meetings I was able to get into as well as the ones I have been able to view because of satellite and the Internet.

A church that may seem quiet and spiritually lacking can by the end of the service be dancing and shouting and clapping and sometimes there will be a Jericho march with people dancing and singing as they march around the church believing for a miracle. They are charismatic and exuberant and it affects the people directly. They don't have a program or an agenda to push. They are ministers of the kingdom and they use the opportunity to energize the people by speaking hope, faith, words of life and imparting their expectancy on God for a miracle.

Thank God for the gift of the Apostle to the Church

I knew the person was God's gift to me in those moments. I hung on every word letting them get into my innermost being. In the services, I would sit on the end of the chair balancing my Bible and pad and pen. These people shaped my life by their radical faith - although mostly I only spoke with them briefly or not at all face to face. These men and women impacted my life causing me to believe for the miraculous and to give my best. The Bible recalls these types of people who are God's to us as heroes of faith:

Hebrews 11: 33 who through faith conquered kingdoms, administered justice, and gained what was promised; who shut the mouths of lions, 34 quenched the fury of the flames, and escaped the edge of the sword; whose weakness was turned to strength; and who became powerful in battle and routed foreign armies.

There were some who were miraculously delivered. Also, there were some who were martyred for their faith. What really happened is that they left their physical body and ascended to be with God. The signs of an Apostle are evident in their spirit, their anointing, their lives (holy set apart for God), their testimonies and their fruit and good works.

Often, thousands of people are in their care. They include congregations close and those in different nations. Because of their travel and global view of the Body of Christ, even though they may start a church or organization, they will often only do it until they train someone to lead and will start fresh elsewhere training up others. They preside; they oversee; that means they keep in communication with a network of churches. People who are trained by them carry a measure of the anointing that was on the apostle. I believe it comes through living close to the person but also through direct impartation of laying on of hands for ministry.

1 Timothy 4: 14 Do not neglect the gift that is in you, which was given to you by prophecy, with the laying on of hands by the elders.

Should you get the opportunity to get into an apostle's meeting, do it. They don't always use the term Apostle so and so. Some do: not all do. The title itself is nothing is there is no fruit such I have described in these pages. The evidence of the tree is in the fruit - Luke 6: 43-46. They speak and their words carry weight and authority beyond themselves. They speak to the body of Christ with God's authority to build up, equip, strengthen and release people in the body of Christ.

Apostles are like Orchestra Conductors

Apostles don't blast into churches and tear down other churches. They usually gather people who desire and need a miracle. Minsters are drawn to them that they may learn how to Shepherd. Prophets desire to be around them because they are inspired and often the two ministry gifts together are like the dynamic duo of the Holy Spirit. The Prophet may see a vision and tell it. The Apostle will get the details and be inspired to release the people who can help to do it. They complement each other in ministry. The apostle knows if a Teacher or a Pastor should be chosen or an Evangelist. The Apostle is like an orchestra conductor who knows how to call the various instruments to play their part so that it is the best possible symphony.

If you can get into an apostle's meetings, do it. Gain all that you possibly can. They teach on various levels. First, their lives are as living epistles; their lives show evidence of the scriptures throughout. They can explain the scriptures by living them. They teach doctrinal truths and foundational truths and bring them to life as though they are as exciting as the miracles themselves. Signs and wonders follow them. Sometimes denominations spring up because of them. They are not confined by denomination. I have known of certain apostles who could preach to Pentecostals or Charismatics but were also able to speak to Anglicans or other denominations.

Usually, Apostles are pastors first; sometimes, they are also Evangelists, teachers and prophets. The distinction of an Apostle is not because he or she wears a name tag that says Apostle. The Apostle feels for the churches and people he or she oversees. I mean they care so deeply that the people are learning the truths of Christ and getting a balanced gospel that reflects God's word. They personally pray for the needs of the pastors and ministry in their spheres of influence. The evidence of the Apostle is in the ministers he or she trains up, the churches or Christian organizations that he or she founds and cares for and the fruit of a godly Christian life.

Chapter end key aspects

1. List 2 or 3 apostles that you personally know of who are making a difference in the Church.
2. List any Apostles you know of from the last century.
3. If you have received a special privilege of hearing an Apostle teach or preach, explain how it affected your life. If you did not, pray asking God to bless that man or woman.

3 PROPHETS

Prophets: Ministry Gifts

Prophets are an important part of the five-fold ministry: Apostles, Prophets, Evangelists, Pastors and Teachers (Ephesians 4: 11). The Apostle Paul emphasizes the gift of prophecy in the following passage. Although he was talking about the gift of prophecy, not the office of prophet, the meaning applies to both.

In 1 Corinthians 14: 18 I thank my God that I speak in tongues more than you all. 19 Yet in the church I had rather speak five words with my understanding, that by my voice I might teach others also, than ten thousand words in an unknown tongue.

Prophets speak words of edification, exhortation and comfort. Edification is building up or strengthening of people. Exhortation is like correction but giving a positive way that encourages people. Comfort are words that bring hope and faith and encouragement to the congregation. Sometimes, they speak words of direction or of warning. In the Old Covenant or Old Testament, prophets heard from God directly and spoke God's words to people including kings, rulers, ordinary people and people who God was choosing to do certain things. Because God's Holy Spirit would come upon a man or woman, he or she would be prompted by God to speak His words to people. They were also called seers because often God would show them things to come. An example would be Daniel because God showed him things that were to happen thousands of years after his life. Some of things have not yet happened.

In the Old Covenant, most people who worshipped God did not speak with God directly. That is God did not speak with all people directly. God used his prophets to convey messages to His people. For instance, Moses was used by God to speak to Israel about their deliverance from Egyptian captivity. Moses also spoke to Pharaoh of Egypt as a chosen spokesperson for God. Prophets were special people who not only loved God but also spoke with God and interceded for ordinary people. The ordinary people would go to the prophet to seek wisdom and answers from God. An example of this is when Samuel is anointed by God to be a prophet and Saul goes to him for help in finding his donkeys.

1 Samuel 9: 6 He said to him, "Look, there is in this city a man of God, and he is highly respected. All that he speaks surely comes about. Now let us go

there. Perhaps he can show us the way that we should go."

Judges 4: 4 Now Deborah, the wife of Lappidoth, was a prophetess. She judged Israel at that time. 5 She would sit under the palm tree of Deborah between Ramah and Bethel in the hill country of Ephraim. The children of Israel would go up to her for her to render judgment.

Deborah gets a specific word from God to give to the Israeli commander Barak.

Moses spoke with God as a man speaks with a friend. He had a special anointing on his life and could speak to God concerning Israel. Most people feared God because they knew God is Holy and they were not. Moses had boldness to speak with God because he was God's chosen representative or prophet.

Exodus 19: 16 So on the third day, in the morning, there was thunder and lightning, and a thick cloud on the mountain, and the sound of an exceedingly loud trumpet. All the people who were in the camp trembled. 17 Then Moses brought the people out of the camp to meet with God, and they stood at the foot of the mountain.

The Prophet Moses

Moses knew God had spoken to him more than once and it gave him boldness to seek God after God miraculously delivered Israel out of Egypt. Moses was the first person God revealed animal sacrifice as a sin offering. God spoke specific instructions on who were to be the priests and the conduct of the priests. Israel did not create a religion based on their own opinions of how to reach God and please him. God instructed Moses in each aspect of worship and life style. There are 613 laws given by which they were to live their lives. They cover worship, marriage and relationships, business, lifestyle, giving, guidelines for every aspect of human life including, law and punishment of offenders. Jehovah God (I AM that I AM as revealed to Moses,) gave the instruction and Moses and the people obeyed. He was an intercessor; he prayed and begged God to have mercy on Israel more than once.

Abraham

Abraham was the first known prophet because God called him out of UR of the Chaldees to go to a country that God would bring him to. God gave him relationship with Himself.

Genesis 12: 1 Now the Lord said to Abram, "Go from your country, your family, and your father's house to the land that I will show you.
2 I will make of you a great nation;
   I will bless you
and make your name great,
   so that you will be a blessing.
3 I will bless them who bless you
   and curse him who curses you,[a]
and in you all families of the earth
   will be blessed."

Abraham obeyed God. It must have been a strong instruction that convinced Abraham to leave all his family, his successful life and go to a place God would show him. That means God told him to go, but did not name the place. God told him to obey and God would direct him in his ways. God did as he promised. The study of Abraham's life will reveal God showing Abraham symbols of God's covenant with him and God's promises that his children's children would be as plentiful as the stars in the sky or grains of sand on a beach. Those who went with Abraham were blessed. God promised that He would bless him and those who were good to him and fight against his enemies. Abraham was given important information by God about circumcision as a sign of covenant with God. Abraham had a miraculous life so that he and his wife had children in their 90's. Isaac and Jacob who was later called Israel were the descendants of Abraham.

For a detailed study on the covenants of God, please see my book on God of Covenant: God's Relationship with Man.

Samuel

Hanna was a God fearing woman who wanted a child. She prayed and fasted that she might have a child and she vowed to give the child to God for his service if she were to conceive. God answered her prayer and she kept her vow. She kept Samuel at home until she had weaned him and brought him as a child to the Temple so that He might be raised by the priests and dedicate his life to serving God.

1 Samuel 1: 24 When she had weaned him, she took him up with her with three bulls, one ephah[b] of flour, and a bottle of wine. And she brought him to the house of the Lord in Shiloh, though the boy was young. 25 Then they slaughtered a bull, and they brought the boy to Eli. 26 And she said,

"Oh, my lord! As you live, my lord, I am the woman that stood by you here praying to the Lord. 27 For this boy I prayed, and the Lord has given me my petition which I asked of Him. 28 Therefore also I have let the Lord have him. As long as he lives he will be dedicated to the Lord." And he worshipped the Lord there.

Samuel was only a boy but he could hear God's voice speaking with him. He did not even know it was God. It was as though he heard an audible voice. Eli the priest teaches him that it is God's voice and what to do should God speak with him.

1 Samuel 3: 7 Now Samuel did not yet know the Lord, nor had the word of the Lord been revealed to him.

8 The Lord again called Samuel a third time. So he arose and went to Eli and said, "Here I am, for you called me."

Then Eli understood that the Lord was calling to the boy. 9 Therefore Eli said to Samuel, "Go, lie down. And it will be, if He calls you, that you will say, 'Speak, Lord, for Your servant listens.' " So Samuel went and lay down in his place.

Samuel had excellent training for ministry living with the priests and he knew God's voice. Later Samuel is known for being a righteous man and living his life wholly pleasing to God all the days of his life. He is used to anoint the first king of Israel. The prophet was the main leader of the people until there were kings.

God reveals who to choose as king to the prophet Samuel. 1 Samuel 9: 17 When Samuel saw Saul, the Lord said to him, "Here is the man of whom I spoke to you! This one will rule over My people."

The Prophets

God gave Samuel specific instructions and Samuel obeyed. A pattern with all the prophets is that they heard God's voice instructing them and some of them saw visions. They were obedient to what God had spoken to them. All of the prophets had supernatural encounters with God. None of them simply served God with no communication. God spoke to each of them. God's instructions were specific and they impacted all of Israel. A true prophet of God would speak a word and it would happen as he or she said it would because the person was giving a message from God to the people.

There were also false prophets. They were people who spoke either through false gods or who spoke saying God said but God didn't say. God instructed Moses how to deal with them.

Deuteronomy 18: 22 When a prophet speaks in the name of the Lord, if the thing does not occur or come to pass, that is the thing which the Lord has not spoken; the prophet has spoken it presumptuously. You shall not be afraid of him.

False Prophets

False prophets who were strong leaders and could gather people to speak lies to were to be put to death.

Deuteronomy 13: 1 If a prophet or a dreamer of dreams arises among you and gives you a sign or a wonder, 2 and the sign or the wonder comes to pass concerning that which he spoke to you, saying, "Let us go after other gods," which you have not known, "and let us serve them," 3 you must not listen to the words of that prophet or that dreamer of dreams, for the Lord your God is testing you, to know whether you love the Lord your God with all your heart and with all your soul. 4 You must follow after the Lord your God, fear Him, and keep His commandments, obey His voice, and you must serve Him, and cling to Him. 5 That prophet or that dreamer of dreams must be put to death because he has spoken in order to turn you away from the Lord your God, who brought you out of the land of Egypt and redeemed you out of the house of bondage, to entice you away from the way in which the Lord your God commanded you to walk. So you must put the evil away from your midst.

The prophet was someone who spoke to the people directly from God. They were well respected and cherished. God's blessing was on Israel when the prophets spoke and Israel lived in line with God's words to them.

Deuteronomy 18: 18 I will raise up a prophet from among their brothers, like you, and will put My words in his mouth, and he will speak to them all that I command him. 19 It will be that whoever will not listen to My words which he will speak in My name, I will require it of him. 20 But the prophet, who presumes to speak a word in my name, which I have not commanded him to speak, or who shall speak in the name of other gods—that prophet shall die."

Prophets were abused

Some prophets were abused, persecuted and martyred because they spoke God's word. A true prophet would say what God wanted him or her to say without being swayed by the people or the rulers who were living in sin. An example of this is the prophet Jeremiah who was thrown into prison and into a miry pit because he spoke the truth of what was to happen to Israel if Israel did not repent.

Jeremiah 32: 1 The word that came to Jeremiah from the Lord in the tenth year of Zedekiah king of Judah, which was the eighteenth year of Nebuchadnezzar. 2 For then the king of Babylon's army besieged Jerusalem, and Jeremiah the prophet was shut up in the court of the prison, which was in the house of the king of Judah.

Even though the king believed that Jeremiah could be speaking the truth, he feared the people and his other wise men more than God. He spoke to Jeremiah secretly. A separate study that could be completed is of all of the kings of Israel who feared people more than God. They knew it probably God speaking, but they feared the people and obeyed their false prophets.

Jeremiah 37: 16 For Jeremiah had entered the dungeon, that is, the vaulted cell, and Jeremiah had remained there many days. 17 Then Zedekiah the king sent and took him out; and the king asked him secretly in his house, and said, "Is there any word from the Lord?"

True prophets of God

True prophets of God do not lie or "say that God said if God didn't say". True prophets of God feared God much more than men at the peril of their own lives. The office of prophet was established by God. The prophet would sometimes be told to live their lives as an example of what God would do. For example, with Ezekiel God instructed him to do certain strange things to get the attention of people of Israel who were not serving God or honouring Him.

Ezekiel 12:5 Dig a hole through the wall in their sight, and go out thereby. 6 In their sight you shall bear it on your shoulders and carry it out in the twilight. You shall cover your face so that you cannot see the land. For I have set you as a sign to the house of Israel.

7 I did so as I was commanded. I brought out my baggage by day as baggage for captivity, and in the evening I dug through the wall with my own hands. I brought it out at twilight, carrying it on my shoulder in their sight.

8 In the morning the word of the Lord came to me, saying: 9 Son of man, has not the house of Israel, the rebellious house, said to you, "What are you doing?"

10 Say to them, "Thus says the Lord God: This oracle concerns the prince in Jerusalem and all the house of Israel who are in it." 11 Say, "I am your sign.

"As I have done, so it shall be done to them. They shall go into exile, into captivity."

As people sinned as disobeyed God, Prophets were mocked, hated, abused and martyred. An example of this is John the Baptist who Jesus says is the greatest prophet who lived.

Matthew 11: 11 Truly I say to you, among those who are born of women, there has risen no one greater than John the Baptist.

The Importance of John the Baptist

I don't believe Jesus was saying he was more important because he was the best prophet but because he was the prophet who announced the coming of the Messiah and who recognized Jesus as the lamb of God who came to take away the sins of the world. John was the forerunner or the one pointing the way to Jesus in Jesus's life. John the Baptist who had called the people of Israel to repent and follow God because the Messiah was coming, recognizes and points to the Messiah and God confirms to him in the view of the people that Jesus Christ is the Messiah.

John 1: 29 The next day John saw Jesus coming toward him and said, "Look, the Lamb of God, who takes away the sin of the world. 30 This is He of whom I said, 'After me comes a Man who is preferred before me, for He was before me.' 31 I did not know Him, but for this reason I came baptizing with water: so that He might be revealed to Israel."

32 Then John bore witness, saying, "I saw the Spirit descending from heaven like a dove, and it remained on Him. 33 I did not know Him, but He who sent me to baptize with water said to me, 'The One on whom you

see the Spirit descending and remaining, this is He who baptizes with the Holy Spirit.' 34 I have seen and have borne witness that He is the Son of God."

Prophets in the New Testament

At no point does God stop calling prophets to function. In fact, God reemphasizes the importance of prophets as he names prophecy as an important manifestational gift: one who prophesies to build up the church with exhortation, edification and comfort; also, God also emphasizes the motivation of prophesy as it is listed in the motivational gift list in 1 Corinthians 12.

1 Corinthians 12: 7 But the manifestation of the Spirit is given to everyone for the common good. 8 To one is given by the Spirit the word of wisdom, to another the word of knowledge by the same Spirit, 9 to another faith by the same Spirit, to another gifts of healings by the same Spirit, 10 to another the working of miracles, to another prophecy, to another discerning of spirits, to another various kinds of tongues, and to another the interpretation of tongues. 11 But that one and very same Spirit works all these, dividing to each one individually as He will.

A motivation is a strong reason to live that shapes your life's direction. Also, finally the office of prophet is mentioned as one of the five-fold ministry gifts.

Ephesians 4: 11 He gave some to be apostles, prophets, evangelists, pastors, and teachers, 12 for the equipping of the saints, for the work of service, and for the building up of the body of Christ, 13 until we all come into the unity of the faith and of the knowledge of the Son of God, into a complete man, to the measure of the stature of the fullness of Christ, 14 so we may no longer be children, tossed here and there by waves and carried about with every wind of doctrine by the trickery of men, by craftiness with deceitful scheming.

For a complete teaching on the manifestational and motivational gifts of prophecy, please see my book on Spiritual Gifts: Knowing them and Using Them. For the purposes of this book, I will only briefly describe the gifts.

Manifestational gift of Prophecy – By the Baptism of the Holy Spirit, God can and desires to use people to speak to encourage, build up and strengthen his people. There could be many people who God uses to prophesy with the manifestational gift of prophecy. What happens is that as the Holy Spirit is given freedom and welcomed in a church or gathering of 2 or more Christians, God inspires someone to speak words. Usually, they are scriptures but sometimes they are encouraging words that are positive affirmations of God's love towards His people. The person who prophesies may do it only occasionally and perhaps be motivated by the gift of Teaching or Leadership. The person might prophesy every week. A regular supernatural occurrence we should expect as Christians is for God to speak to us as we gather to honour Jesus. He uses us, members of the Body of Christ to strengthen the other parts of the Body of Christ around us.

Motivational Gift of Prophesy – The person motivated by prophesy has a different dimension to his or her relationship with God. That is he or she speaks with God and hears from God in a strong intimate way. God shares His heart with that person and often sends the prophet to speak words of encouragement to people. It may not be in a church setting; it could be a church setting.

God usually uses this person in strong intercessory prayer for his or her city or region or country. Some prophets intercede and pray for different parts of the world, because God impresses those places upon the person's heart. The person motivated by prophesy usually has had a supernatural encounter with God and knows he or she is doing what God instructed him or her to do. Much like Moses who knew he should go to Egypt, those motivated by prophesy know they are to do certain things or care for certain people or regions. They are as watchmen.

Habakkuk 2: 2 I will stand at my watch
    and station myself on the watchtower;
and I will keep watch to see what He will say to me,
    and what I will answer when I am reproved.

Watchmen were as guards who cared for their region. They would sound an alarm if anything were to threaten his or her region. Motivational prophets are often praying and interceding for a region of people and contact others for the purposes of keeping the region safe and turning the hearts of people towards God.

The Office of Prophet

The person motivated by prophecy may or may not ever be in the office of prophet. The office of Prophet is not just a name tag that says Prophet. An example often used to describe the five-fold ministry is the human hand. Five fingers – the apostles, prophets, evangelists, teachers and pastor. The forefinger is usually the representation of the prophet as he or she points the way for others. The person speaks God's word of direction. As Moses was chosen by God and recognized by the people, as John the Baptist was chosen by God and acknowledged by the people, so is the Prophet chosen by God and acknowledged by the people. The person is not only motivated by prophesy, but is also living a life of regular supernatural events and occurrences. The person most certainly has supernatural occurrences with God, sometimes with angels and demons. The person prays over his or her territory as revealed by God to him or her. The person serves God by serving the people. Literally people realize there is an authority in the person's words that is the authority of God.

A Prophet can often release giftings of the Holy Spirit within other people or impart them to others. This person certainly prophesies in Church but also uses the gifts of words of wisdom, words of knowledge, discerning of spirits regularly whether in church or out of it. The person may dream dreams that speak to him or her. The dreams are prophetic about the past, present or future. The person may see visions. The person may be an example to the people as Jeremiah was to the people of Israel. That is the person may be experiencing something that is significant not only for himself or herself but for all of those within his or her territory. The person is a living witness of Jesus Christ.

Prophetic Preaching

The person with the office of prophet is recognized as a prophet by other prophets, 1 Corinthians 14: 32. Prophetic preaching is unlike any other type of preaching. Prophetic preaching is not simply a Bible study, as important as they are. The person gets a word from God directly to give to a group of people. The person is inspired to preach a RHEMA Word or a quickened Word. The word preached impacts the congregation in a supernatural way.

I have been privileged to receive preaching from true prophets of God. What occurs is that the words they preach piece the very core of your spirit. The Holy Spirit within you leaps at the words knowing it is exactly what God is saying to you. The person rejoices with the word of God preached so strongly it may motivate the person to give generously to people or the church or the prophet. It may encourage the person to give of their efforts or service, of finances, of the treasures of the Holy Spirit within him or her. The RHEMA Word or quickened word by the Holy Spirit is energized by faith; it is received by faith; it produces supernatural spiritual results – it results in action whether it is giving, repenting, praying for something or someone etc.

I have been privileged to be a part of a church where the Pastor was also a strong prophet of God. This is not a usual combination of giftings. What would happen is the Pastor would preach sermons that radically changed people's lives. Often, Pastor Loren would stop, in his sermon and get a word of wisdom or a word of knowledge about someone in the congregation. He would call that person or that family to come forward and he would give a word of prophecy to that person or persons and they often would either kneel down and begin praising God or be slain in the Spirit. Sometimes as he was praying over people at the end of the service he would start speaking in tongues really strongly and be prophesying in Spanish (at that point in his life he did not know Spanish).

I am saying that a Prophet of God can say words that can so impact the spirit of a person that they literally cause the person to be transformed. It may include an outward evidence such as being slain in the spirit or immediately kneeling or lying face down on the carpet. It invokes Godly fear and reverence and the person or people that God is revealing the secret things of a person's heart.

1 Corinthians 14: 24 But if all prophesy and there comes in one who does not believe or one unlearned, he is convinced by all and judged by all. 25 Thus the secrets of his heart are revealed. And so falling down on his face, he will worship God and report that God is truly among you.

I have witnessed many such occurrences of people kneeling or bowing or lying prostrate on the ground as a prophet of God speaks words that only God and the person know about. There is an overwhelming sense of God's presence and His care over secret things, things a person may not even mention to anyone but God cares about all aspects of His people. God can unlock spiritual gifts in people or identify giftings in people. The person himself or herself will be in agreement with the words being spoken.

A gift that was dormant may be quickened and brought to significance. It brings release to a person. God demonstrates Himself in this way usually to comfort the people and to confirm what they already knew, but also sometimes letting them know He is separating them for a purpose. If you are hearing the prophetic word, let faith ignite in your heart; stir yourself up and claim those promises of God for your own self so that the word mixed with faith can produce life in you.

Although I attended that church several years, and I witnessed hundreds of personal prophecies, I did not get called out specifically for a word. I didn't miss out on one blessing though, because if someone went forward to receive prophecy, I grabbed onto it in my spirit and prayed " O God let that word be unto me. Let my faith be combined with that word that the blessings of it can also be for me."

Recognize the gift: Receive from the person's giftings

Should you receive or have opportunity to receive from a prophet of God, get as much as you can by releasing your faith. I am saying pray in agreement with the prophet of God for the people. Also, claim those blessings for yourself. Say to God, 'Yes God I agree. Let me also receive in that area.' I believe God honours your faith. If you come into agreement with the prophecies of others and also claim them as your own, God will honour your faith. You can inherit by faith those same blessings. When a prophet of God prays or exhorts a congregation, grab onto those promises for yourself. Release your faith to receive from the servant of God. The reason I believe you can grab onto the promises of God, even if the prophet isn't directly speaking to you, is because I have done so. Also, it is scriptural.

A Canaanite woman begged Jesus to heal her daughter but Jesus answers her roughly saying the promises are for the Jews and she is like a Gentile dog. This is about the most horrible insult he could say to her. Yet the woman still believes because she recognizes he is God's servant. She pleads for mercy – that even the dogs can get crumbs from the table. She identifies that yes she is a Gentile but she believes.

Matthew 15: 21 Then Jesus went from there and departed into the regions of Tyre and Sidon. 22 There, a woman of Canaan came out of the same regions and cried out to Him, saying, "Have mercy on me, O Lord, Son of David. My daughter is severely possessed by a demon."

23 But He did not answer her a word. And His disciples came and begged Him, saying, "Send her away, for she cries out after us."

24 But He answered, "I was sent only to the lost sheep of the house of Israel."

25 Then she came and worshipped Him, saying, "Lord, help me."

26 But He answered, "It is not fair to take the children's bread and to throw

it to dogs."

27 She said, "Yes, Lord, yet even dogs eat the crumbs that fall from their masters' table."

Because this woman believed and would not stop believing, she received a miracle for her daughter. Jesus says to her the following:

Matthew 15: 28 Then Jesus answered her, "O woman, great is your faith. Let it be done for you as you desire." And her daughter was healed instantly. That woman believed in Jesus before He was glorified (risen from the dead); how much more it applies to us today who have been made one in Christ because of Jesus blood. We can inherit the promises of God by faith (Hebrews 6: 12)

Humility

A true Prophet if God is humble, knowing only God can give the word as it comes. The person doesn't fall into the pit of pride believing he or she is an excellent preacher or speaker. The person delivers God's Word and gives God all the glory. Similar to the prophets who demonstrated with their lives the intervention of God, those with the office of prophet may live lives that show things to many people. The significance of a word or action may impact the lives of others.

A true prophet of God cares about God and God's word more than any people or persons. A true prophet of God will never contradict the Word of God. That means in no way will the words be contrary to the Holy Scriptures which reveal to us how to live our lives. If someone says something not scriptural it could be the person is ignorant of God's Word and should be corrected; or it could mean the person is deceived in sin and is a false prophet. Usually a prophet of God will either directly quote God's word to a person or paraphrase the scriptures with his or her own words. It is almost always true that a prophet will quote or paraphrase Scripture, but certainly his or her words will never contradict scripture.

False Prophets

An example of a false prophet destroying lives was the horrible thing that happened at Jonestown. There was a false prophet who gathered together thousands of people and had them all killed by drinking poison. Also, there have been other cults where the leader lives in adultery or in polygamy and makes up his or her own rules – not following the word of

God. Pray that God would give you discerning of spirits strong and always use the Word of God as the plumb line. The plumb line is the line that is straight. It is often used by carpenters as a guide for installing walls or other important structures. The Word of God is always correct. There may be false prophets. Do not be deceived by them. You won't be if God's word if first always. No personal prophecy can ever contradict God's Word and be true. Jesus warns us that there will be false prophets.

Matthew 7: 15 "Beware of false prophets who come to you in sheep's clothing, but inwardly they are ravenous wolves. 16 You will know them by their fruit. Do men gather grapes from thorns, or figs from thistles? 17 Even so, every good tree bears good fruit. But a corrupt tree bears evil fruit.

The Fruit is the Proof

If the fruit is the proof, those who live by the Word of God will keep the Word of God as the authority of all of life. Their lives will align with the scriptures. False prophets gather people for selfish gain and their lives will be sinful. Usual ways a person strays from God is in pride, sexual sin, covetousness. If someone tells you that you can pay to get a prophesy, have nothing to do with that person. God's gifts are given freely. If someone tells you that you can pay for your sins to be erased, have nothing to do with him or her. The gift of prophesy is not for financial gain; it is a free gift of Jesus Christ to the Church of Jesus Christ. Only Jesus blood can forgive sins. We can never earn a gift or a word from God. Jesus commanded his disciples:

Matthew 10: 8 Heal the sick, cleanse the lepers, raise the dead, and cast out demons. Freely you have received, freely give.

Areas of Caution for all ministers

A true prophet can go off of he or she is ensnared by pride. They would believe they are special because they are elite and they fail to give God the glory. Those who follow these false prophets are in a pathway that will lead to destruction. Sexual immorality can come if a man or woman doesn't remain sexually pure. Often people worship the prophets themselves and will be willing to do anything to get near them. This is not a right attitude towards the ministry. If a prophet is not wise, he or she may give into sexual immorality and damage many people because of it. Covetousness or the love of money and financial wealth becomes most important to that person. It is not wrong to be wealthy. It is wrong to love wealth more than God or people. It is never correct to make people pay for

God's giftings.

An example of it can be with Simon the sorcerer who got saved but had a perversion towards money. The apostle Paul strictly rebukes him for this sin.

Acts 8: 18 When Simon saw that through the laying on of the apostles' hands the Holy Spirit was given, he offered them money, 19 saying, "Give me also this power, that whomever I lay hands on may receive the Holy Spirit."

20 Peter said to him, "May your money perish with you, because you thought you could purchase the gift of God with money! 21 You have neither part nor share in this matter, for your heart is not right before God. 22 Therefore repent of your wickedness, and ask God if perhaps the intention of your heart may be forgiven you. 23 For I see that you are in the gall of bitterness and in the bond of iniquity."

The only way a Christian can know the difference between a true prophet and a false prophet is by the fruit. This is only possible through discerning of spirits. Pray for discerning of spirits to be strong in you. Also, read as much of the Word of God as you can in every opportunity that you can. The word of God sharpens our discernment. The Word of God clearly shows the truth to those who seek God. The truth of God's Word is always the final word.

In some countries today, they are persecuted and martyred because they speak and preach God's Word. Often their lives are as examples to the people around them, The Prophet person has unshakable faith in God and is strongly moved with the gift of faith because he or she can see what God wants to do and it is impossible without God's intervention.

A True Prophet of God Must Speak What God says

A true prophet of God will only speak what God says. The person will not add extra words or subtract words for selfish gain. Even though Balaam is prophet of God, he is covetous. He wants the money he is offered to curse Israel. In Numbers 23-24, Balaam says he will only speak what God says and although he seeks God for a word to curse Israel, as the king would pay him richly for doing, he does not. He says only what God says about Israel. I am not stating this to show that Balaam is a desirable character. I am showing that even though he was perverted by covetousness, he did not say words that God didn't say.

When Naaman the leper is healed at the word of Elisha, Elisha takes no gift from him. Sometimes, prophets took gifts from people, but on this occasion, Elisha believed he should take nothing. Gehazi, his servant was full of covetousness and saw an opportunity to make some money for himself by lying. He sneaks away and fins Naaman and asks for gifts; he lies and says it is the word of his master Elisha.

2 Kings 5: 20 Then Gehazi the servant of Elisha the man of God said, "My master has spared Naaman the Aramean by not taking from his hands what he brought. As the Lord lives, I will run after him and take something from him."

21 So Gehazi pursued Naaman. Then Naaman saw him running after him, jumped down from the chariot to meet him, and said, "Is everything all right?"

22 And he said, "Everything is all right. My master has sent me and says, 'Even now two servants from Ephraim, from the sons of the prophets, have come to me. Give them a talent[c] of silver and two changes of clothes.'"

Please notice, Gehazi isn't saying that God said it, only that Elisha the prophet said it. He was lying for selfish gain. Elisha curses Gehazi for it. I believe the reason is that God wanted Naaman to take the message of the healing power of the God of Israel to his country. God would freely heal because of obedience and faith.

Elisha is shown (by God) what Gehazi did.

2 Kings 5: 25 Then he entered and stood before his master. And Elisha said to him, "Where have you come from, Gehazi?"
And he said, "Your servant went here and there."

26 He said to him, "Did my heart not go with you when the man turned from his chariot to meet you? Is it a time to take money, and to take garments, olives and vineyards, sheep and oxen, male and female servants? 27 The leprosy of Naaman will cling to you and to your descendants forever." So he went out from his presence, leprous like snow.

A true prophet of God will never take gifts as payment for a miracle or a healing. The true prophet of God will know when to receive a blessing from someone and when someone's heart is not right.

Only what God says

A true prophet of God should only speak what God says even if embellishing it a bit would make it stronger. The prophet must control his or her own tongue. I literally have been corrected by God for embellishing something to make it sound more appealing. It is lying if it is anything beyond what God has said. O the true prophet of God would know that what God says is most important and those words could make a difference to the person igniting faith or releasing a blessing. Anything people add to God's words is sin. Anything withheld that is God's word is sin. God is the reprove of those who do such things. Prophets must learn to discern the difference between saying God's words and other words that rise up.

As a prophet is learning, he or she must learn how to recognize what God is clearly saying compared to what seems to be the best words according to the human soul. There is a fine line there of what God says and what a person wants to say because they are words that come from the soul. Remember the soul is the mind, will and emotions of a person. God's gifts flow through the Holy Spirit, through our spirit – not from the soul realm. To be used by God we must empty ourselves of ourselves and only say what God says.

Isaiah 6: 5 And I said: "Woe is me! For I am undone because I am a man of unclean lips, and I dwell in the midst of a people of unclean lips. For my eyes have seen the King, the Lord of Hosts."

6 Then one of the seraphim flew to me with a live coal which he had taken with the tongs from off the altar in his hand. 7 And he laid it on my mouth, and said, "This has touched your lips, and your iniquity is taken away, and your sin purged."

If you want to add something to what God has said to you make it clear and say this is what God says exactly. Then use your mouth to say I believe it means this… and give your own meaning. Do not say God said it if he didn't. Even the apostle Paul did it. As he preached on reasons for remaining single, he admitted it was his recommendation not God's word. It was important to the Christians of his generation because there was persecution of Christians.

1 Corinthians 7: 6 I speak this as a concession and not as a command. 7 For I would that all men were even as I myself. But every man has his proper gift from God, one after this manner and another after that.

Signs and Wonders

There are signs and wonders that follow a Prophet of God. An example of this century could be William Branham. He had many miraculous supernatural dealings with God and was used mightily by God in the 1950's to bring words of wisdom and words of knowledge and discerning of spirits to people and through these gifts, people's lives were radically transformed. People were healed; people received miracles. Sometimes, people would come forward to be prayed for and he would get a word of wisdom or a word of knowledge about the person's and say " You were doing this thing with these people and such and such" He could tell them secret things that only they knew. They would respond by being overwhelmed with God's presence and often fall the ground and be completely healed.

Some people received miracles; some people received answers to prayers; some people were healed; some people were able to believe God. I believe he was a true prophet of God but what happened later in his life is that pride took root in him and he began to go off in doctrinal error and no person corrected him because the people almost worshipped him instead of God. Although there was a true calling of God, there was departure from the scriptures. God will never contradict his Word. God will never speak things contrary to the written word of God.

Renown

God will often raise a prophet to a position of authority and influence within his or her nation. For example, all of the prophets were known by the kings of Israel and also by other nations. They were either loved or hated depending on if the king was following God's Word or living in idolatry. God often instructed the prophets to speak certain things to the leaders.

For example, Elisha the prophet would get words of knowledge and words of wisdom about what was going on in the place of not only Israel but also the enemy nations. There was belief that perhaps there was a traitor in the ranks in the King or Aram's troops. Even the enemy army knew that God spoke to the prophet in Israel.

2 Kings 5: 11 The mind of the king of Aram was troubled by this, so he called his servants and said to them, "Will you not tell me who among us sides with the king of Israel?"

12 Then one of his servants said, "No one, my lord, O king. Elisha, the prophet who is in Israel, tells the king of Israel the words that you speak in your bedroom."

The secret things of other nations were revealed to the prophets. Elisha could advise the king on what to do concerning military matters because of what showed him. Elisha's words were the words God gave him, so Israel would achieve victory.

The Secret Things

Deuteronomy 29: 29 The secret things belong to the Lord our God, but those things which are revealed belong to us and to our children forever, so that we may keep all the words of this law.

It is the same God who can give His prophets words of wisdom, words of knowledge and words to bring in certain situations where we have no natural knowledge. God can give us words that help to radically intervene bringing an answer to prayer should we speak them.

The value of a true prophet of God to a ruler to only say what God says could impact a nation for God and lead to success and prosperity. A true ruler will not only have natural advisers in matters of ruling a country or kingdom, but have spiritual advisors who can give him or her wisdom from God.

Gathering of the Prophets

There is an excitement when a prophet of God is going to preach a service. The people are expecting the miraculous. Faith is in the atmosphere. There is a desire to hear from God and also an excitement about what God is going to do. Should there be a gathering of prophets, the atmosphere is so full of the gift of faith, there may be trembling; there may be people slain in the Spirit. There may be an outpouring of the manifestational gift of prophecy. There is a unique dynamic is a true prophetic gathering. God is going to speak to the people through His prophets and it is going to transform not only the present meeting but the lives of those there. The Prophets together energize each other. They do not compete; they complement each other and they are inspired and encouraged by each other so they seem to be more effective.

Should you have opportunity to get in a gathering of the prophets of God, get in it. You will not regret it. God will manifest himself in that meeting. I have been in meetings where prophets preach and prophesy and people will often receive healing, deliverance, life callings, miracles, life changes. I am talking about radical life changing decisions that can occur. I am not even talking about personal prophesy – only the atmosphere and the gathering of prophets.

In a gathering of prophets, you can learn what is appropriate, what is not; you can learn what different impressions mean and how to verbalize the, You can use the gift of prophecy more freely because faith for prophecy is in the atmosphere. You can discern what the more mature prophets are doing. It is the best way for a prophet to develop. Get into meetings of prophets. At my church where pastor Loren is a prophet, we had a school of the prophets. There was teaching on what is and what is not correct. The Scripture was the main textbook. I thank God for that class that made a huge impact on my life by helping me develop my giftings.

The only one

If you are the only prophet in your church, you have got to connect to other prophets in some way. Read books; go to conferences. Learn all you can. The proper way it should be is that the elder prophets teach the new ones. You must learn how to use your gift. The Holy Spirit of course is your main teacher, but experienced prophets can share, with you truths that other people do not understand. Once more, I thank God for Christian Broadcasting. There is Christian television, cable stations, satellite and Prophets on the Internet. There is no reason that you cannot connect with other prophets in some way.

There are known prophets of God who travel throughout North America and other countries who can give you instruction. Their books, CD's DVD's and websites give much information. Pray about who you should be listening to. God usually makes an automatic connection between a preacher and the audience. The same happens with prophets. Never believe you cannot learn or be taught. God can use Christians to sharpen each other as metal sharpens metal.

Submit to authority

A prophet in a church must come in submission to the leadership of the church. This is essential. Prophets who know they have a word from God, if not taught proper decorum, may blurt out a prophesy in the wrong moment or without the Pastor's approval. A prophet must be subject to the leadership of the meeting he or she is in. I have seen prophets who blurt out of order ad are corrected publically. I have seen prophets muffled and silenced by leadership that did not approve of them even though their message was exactly what God wanted to speak. If the word was from God, the leadership must answer to God for not allowing the prophecy.

The true prophet of God must respect authority and submit to it. If he or she can not submit, he or she should go to a different church. If you cannot submit to the authority in your church, meet with the pastor and speech to him or her. If you know you can accept the leadership after a meeting such as this, do the best thing – leave the church. Go to the right place you belong. Prophets are not to compete with pastors – they are to assist and compliment them.

If you are corrected by the pastor for a prophecy and don't know why, go directly to the pastor afterwards and ask the reason. The pastor or minister leading the service must watch over the people and care for them. They must give account of what they let be said over those people. I have been in services where the pastor has corrected a prophecy and it was true. There was a strong witness in my spirit saying – yes that word was too harsh or it exposed a sin. It was not appropriate for a public service.

If it were you who was corrected, take correction as a way of learning the difference between speaking from the spirit or speaking from the soul. Receive it and ask God to help you. It can be a learning experience for you. Spiritual gifts grow and develop by exercising them. You must use your gift in order to use it properly. Let your heart be pure and receive the best you can from the experience. If you keep your heart pure, God can teach you and you can be used by God. You must remain humble and teachable.

The Five-fold ministry goal

The five-fold ministry is suppose to work together as the fingers on a hand The apostle, prophet, evangelist, pastor, and teacher. Should you be in the right place with the right people, the pastor will be welcoming of the prophets. The Apostle will help to bring the word to come by organizing people to make it happen. The Evangelists will contribute. The teachers will be studying the scriptures and teaching the people. The ministry team will flow together and there will be total smooth action. An example is that I may use my hand – the five fingers to hold an object or to let go. The human hand can do many amazing things. If one finger is not responding properly or more than one, you can use your hand as smoothly. You cannot do what you would like to accomplish. God wants the five-fold ministry to flow together to all join together to build up and strengthen the church so that all members of the church are taught and used to bring salvation, healing and deliverance to others.

If a prophetic word comes to the congregation, the response should be the whole church prays. I have been a part of some churches where the word of prophecy was highly regarded and all the church would pray immediately after it. Some people would go to the altar. Some people would get on their knees to receive. The church body should respond to a prophetic word. The prophetic word brings life and God's encouragement and strengthening to the church. Often those in the office of prophet will get a word about the future of a church or of people within the church.

Amos 3: 7 7 Surely the Lord God does nothing
    without revealing His purpose
    to His servants the prophets.

Usually, this is not spoken in the general church congregation but is spoken to the pastor and then perhaps announced to the congregation as directed by the pastor. Usually, the congregational prophecy is to encourage, exhort and comfort. If the prophet speaks it to the pastor, it is usually a confirmation of something the pastor was thinking about or believing. It is a confirmation. If you are with the right people, in the right place, prophetic gifting will be honoured and God will use you as part of the leadership. If you are not in the right place or not with the right people, you will not get a free flow for the prophetic and there will be resistance to the prophetic word because it isn't the right place for you.

I compare it to some place you belong such as your home. You've got the key to your home. You can go through the front door. You know where everything is; you know what things are yours. You can't just go to any home on your street and get in with your key. You can't just get in through the front door. You won't own the things in the home. It isn't yours. The best solution is go where you belong and where you are celebrated and treasured. Do not go where they oppose you and resist you.

The people who speak into your life, know them. Not every prophet or minister is meant to be speaking to you or speaking into your life. Be careful of what you hear or listen to. God says he will raise up those in our midst who we know and who know us. There are those who will speak into your life and it will prosper you and strengthen you. There are those are not for you. You may not agree with them or they might not be best for you.

Pray about those you receive from and pray for those you receive from.

Deuteronomy 18: 18 I will raise up a prophet from among their brothers, like you, and will put My words in his mouth, and he will speak to them all that I command him. 19 It will be that whoever will not listen to My words which he will speak in My name, I will require it of him.

Conditional

Prophesy spoken over people, whether it be the congregation or families or individuals is always conditional. It depends on your willingness to believe it and obey it. It depends on you preparing yourself and aligning with the word. It depends on what you do with it. The prophecy doesn't instantly manifest with its hearing. For example, if someone prophesies that the church will be blessed and multiplied in size and a multitude will get saved because of it, but the congregation and the leadership do not receive the word and align with it, they may receive nothing. If they believe the word, they should respond by obeying it. That is, they should begin evangelism. They should do outreaches to win souls.

If a person is prophesied over to receive a ministry but the person runs away and goes the opposite way and ends up in sin and disobedience, that person will have to give account for the giftings he or she had and his or her resistance to God's calling on his or her life. God never forces us to do anything. He may reveal what is best for us, but we always have a choice. If you hear a prophet speak a word and you know it is for you but you disobey or fail to obey, or do nothing, you must answer to God for this because you disobeyed God's instructions to you.

Prophet may withdraw

The prophet is as God's mouth speaking to the church. That can only come through hearing God's voice. There are seasons, when a prophet of God will withdraw from even close family and friends for a period to seek God. Jesus Himself did this often. You may be reading where there were miracles and healings and a multitude who followed him and a verse later see that Jesus went off alone to go pray.

Luke 5: 15 Yet even more so His fame went everywhere. And great crowds came together to hear and to be healed by Him of their infirmities. 16 But He withdrew to the wilderness and prayed.

During the communion with God the person is strengthened and renewed and refreshed and can resume his or her normal life. Prayer and intercession a a strong area of priority to a prophet a God. Direct communion with God is essential not only to share what God is speaking but because the prophet is created in such a way that he or she needs to be with God more. There is like a pulling on the inside of you that you know you should give yourself to prayer and fasting.

Moses, for instance, often withdrew to go speak with God concerning Israel. God was using him but he drew his strength from God. He would go speak with God and it would give him boldness to speak to Pharaoh and also with Israel.

Intercession

The prophet often intercedes for the people in his or her own territory. The best example I can see of this is Moses and Aaron. The people would have been destroyed if not for the intercession and faith of Moses and Aaron who prayed mercy for Israel. If you do not like some prophet's ministry, or any minister's ministry do not gossip about it. God cares what you say about his servants.

If you speak negative things about a minister of God, you sow seeds of unrighteousness or flesh. You will reap what you sow. If you do not like a minister, pray and talk to God about it not other people. I am not talking about someone who is clearly in sin and disobeying the LORD. For instance, the people of Israel would often sin against God and turn their hatred towards Moses and Aaron. In these moments, God would have killed all of them. Moses and Aaron interceded for the people.

Numbers 14: 42 When the assembly was gathered against Moses and Aaron, they looked toward the tent of meeting. The cloud covered it, and the glory of the Lord appeared. 43 Moses and Aaron went before the tent of meeting. 44 And the Lord spoke to Moses, saying, 45 "Get up from among this assembly, that I may destroy them in a moment." And they fell on their faces.

46 Moses said to Aaron, "Take a censer and put fire in it from off the altar, and put in incense, and go quickly to the assembly, and make an atonement for them, because wrath has gone out from the Lord. The plague has begun." 47 Aaron took it as Moses commanded and ran into the midst of the assembly, where the plague had begun among the people. He put in incense and made an atonement for the people. 48 He stood between the dead and the living, and the plague was stopped.

House of Prayer Kansas City

Although often it is not quoted as being a place for prophesy, it is. The praised and worship is prophetic. The intercession is prophetic and the ministry team are prophetic. Prayer is such a high priority in this place that 24/7 someone is praying and worshipping God. It has been this way since 1999. In an atmosphere or praise and worship, often prophecy is released in songs, exhortations, worship etc. Many people in the body of Christ may not understand this church or its priorities. I myself, when I first knew of it in 1999, thought to myself shouldn't they be doing something else? The truth though is I didn't understand as I do now. They evangelize. They feed the hungry; they have a food bank; they have other activities, but the main distinction in them is their desire to pray and be in God's presence. People who flow in the prophetic would feel very comfortable in that church because of the constant worship, praise and prayer – an atmosphere for the prophetic as well as the other gifts of God.

Personal prophecy

Often those motivated by prophesy will get personal words for people. That is, God will speak something to the person that can change the condition of that person's life. It may be an answer to prayer; it may be a release of a gift; it may be a word of knowledge – knowing something that only God and that person know. It may be a word of wisdom – supernatural answer to a problem or situation. God can speak a word through a prophet that revolutionizes the church. Examples can be seen in this last 50 years through Kenneth Hagin, Kenneth Copeland, Bill Hammon, and others. These people not only taught and preached the word of God, they heard God speak and prophesied over people, congregations, regions and even nations.

Excellent books I would recommend on the Prophetic are by Bill Hammon, and Paula Sandford. There are many more but these are the ones that have helped teach me essential truths about the office of Prophet. Pray for spiritual discernment to come strong in your life. Pray that God will give you mentors who will teach you; pray that God will give you divine connections with other prophets of God so that you might learn and that you may develop your gift. Your gift is for the building up of the body of Christ. Use your gift; remain humble; remain teachable that God might use you to edify, exhort, comfort and speak God's word into God's people's lives.

Chapter end questions

1. Name 2 or 3 prophets that you know of in the present Church.
2. If you have never heard prophetic preaching, pray and ask God that you might know what it is.
3. If prophetic preaching has transformed your life explain it; tell someone in your family or close friendships what God has done for you through prophet ministry.

4 EVANGELISTS

Evangelists

Ephesians 4: 11 He gave some to be apostles, prophets, evangelists, pastors, and teachers, 12 for the equipping of the saints, for the work of service, and for the building up of the body of Christ, 13 until we all come into the unity of the faith and of the knowledge of the Son of God, into a complete man, to the measure of the stature of the fullness of Christ,

The Evangelist is a person who has a passion to save souls. This person is motivated by God to care for those who do not know Jesus Christ as Saviour or who have gone away from the LORD. The Evangelist often gets a vision from God of a harvest field. That is the analogy the scripture uses. Jesus imparts his heart for those who are ready but there are no labourers. This very scripture often is so much a part of the Evangelists vision and purpose. He or she knows that Jesus is going to return and there are millions of people who do not yet know Christ. It is the heart of the Evangelist to preach salvation, healing and deliverance to people.

John 4: 35 Do you not say, 'There are yet four months, and then comes the harvest'? Listen! I say to you, lift up your eyes and look at the fields, for they are already white for harvest.

Evangelists of the Century

In this past century, God raised up many evangelists to preach and win souls. If you don't know anything about them but feel a desire to win souls, I recommend you read about these heroes of faith: Smith Wigglesworth, John G. Lake, Amy Semple McPherson, Maria Woodworth-Etter, Billy Graham, Oral Roberts, Lester Sumerall, Benny Hinn, R. W Schambach, Rex Humbard. There are many others. What these people share is that they gave their lives to evangelize. They gave their lives to win souls. Their main priority was preaching and teaching Jesus Christ as Saviour and king. Multitudes were impacted by their ministry. Roberts Liardon has an excellence series of books (God's Generals) about the healing evangelists and also a DVD series. I would highly recommend them. The focus is on what they did for God, what happened to them if they missed God and what we can learn from their lives.

Evangelists preached in open air theatres, on street corners, in fancy churches, and in ordinary places. They preached to one or a small crowd with as much passion as they preached to thousands and thousands. The message is simple. Jesus Christ is the only way for salvation. Often after their preaching signs and wonders followed. What that means is people repented and turned to God; people were healed. People were baptized in the Holy Spirit. People turned to God with all their being. The Evangelists of the last century have transformed North America and other parts of the world. I don't know of any person who doesn't know who Billy Graham is. Even though the people may not be Christians, they will acknowledge and respect Billy Graham because he lived a simple, humble life but travelled and streamed his services on public TV stations winning souls.

The Character of the Evangelists

The Evangelists may have boldness and preach on the streets. My pastor's mentor who trained him in the things of God would often stand up in a restaurant and say out loud "Quiet please. I am going to thank God for our meal" Everyone would be silent. The man would pray and everyone would resume their chatter. He had boldness to do it.

I knew of an Evangelist who would witness to every waitress or service person who waited on him. He was so likable and friendly, he would invite people to come hear him preach and they would go. The evangelist may be more conservative or shy. I knew a senior woman who would share Christ with any person that came to her home to do repairs or construction or any person she met while shopping etc. She used to carry salvation tracts with her and give them to people she met. She could get away with it because she had a beautiful smile and twinkle in her eye, and silver hair. Not too many people could consider her intimidating. I knew of a minister who would come to preach at my church. Where mostly every person who attended was a Christian and after this man preached, the altars would be packed with people giving their lives to God to be used in Evangelism. I myself was so moved by his calling for those who would give their lives for Christ, I almost ran to the altar.

Evangelists Preach no matter what

Joyce Meyer probably doesn't think of herself as an Evangelist; she is an excellent teacher of the gospel but there is a part of her that is and evangelist. I saw her speaking on one of her crusades overseas and the officials in that region wanted to cancel her meetings. They paid much money to travel and to rent the place etc. She wasn't going to cancel. When they didn't work, they tried fear tactics. There were death threats. She still went on with the meeting. There were thousands of people there. What they did is turn off all the electricity on her so the people could not hear her. She grabbed a megaphone and got on top of one of their vehicles and preached anyway to as many as would stay. The people stayed. Even though some could not hear her. She preached the gospel – no matter what. The evangelist has got that sort of drive, I will preach it, because I answer to God.

Other evangelists I've heard of preach during rainstorms. The people sometimes walk for days to get to the meeting. The people stay in the rain. The evangelist will minister in any condition. Gloria Copeland was preaching in a large church and there was a terrible storm. She kept preaching. The roof of the building was literally torn off the top of the building. Gloria Copeland continued preaching. The people stayed to receive the preaching. They prayed about the storm and commanded it to leave. That boldness to preach Christ no matter what may happen is an aspect of the Evangelist that is most like Christ. Jesus preached and taught at even at the death threats and hatred of the Pharisees.

A vision of the destiny of the sinner

Most of the evangelists I have had opportunity to hear preach either in person or on TV had some encounter with God that gave them a zeal to win souls. They often envision those who are away from the LORD and can see their destiny as hell. It so deeply moves the evangelist, he or she will dedicate his or her life to sharing Christ. Not all of the Evangelists I've known of have had advanced education; some have; some have not. Their character traits include a strong desire to use all means of communication to win souls. Their desire is to tell as many people about Jesus Christ as possible.

Several decades ago, there was a meeting of Evangelists that involved targeting the 10/40 window. Those are the longitude and latitude numbers that include the highest number of people who are not Christians. Many of them have had no opportunity to hear the gospel of Jesus Christ let alone accept him as Saviour and Lord. Many ministries target these unreached people groups to share Christ with them. Youth With a Mission and Christ For the Nations are two major organizations that are known to training, equipping and sending ministers to preach Christ.

Often, we in North America forget that in some nations Christians are persecuted and martyred because of their unjust government systems. The

Evangelists will target those regions. For example, in North Korea where people are often killed for their Christian faith, Youth With a Mission is recruiting people who will go, even if they are imprisoned or martyred. They are secretly brought in and may never get out. The people agree to go because they know there may be no other Christian ministers in that place. They know they may never leave the country but they will give their lives hoping to reach those for Christ.

I have known of Evangelist that have had their lives threatened if they were to preach their evangelistic Crusades. The Evangelists, prayed, committed themselves to God and continued with the meetings. In some countries, Evangelists can in no way openly preach so they meet with the underground church and share Christ with them and encourage them building them up in faith. In such situations, they bring healing and deliverance messages as many Christians in those countries don't have much knowledge of Scripture because rarely can they keep a Bible without it being taken away from them.

Evangelists believe they are accountable to God

Something that drives the Evangelist to preach is they personally feel that if they do not do all they can to reach souls, they will be held responsible for it. Part of it comes from a supernatural encounter with God that quickens them and gives them the passion and the direction to evangelize. Certain Christian denominations are more given to evangelism than others. I would include missions in evangelism although many evangelists feel called to a country or a region, some travel the world; some preach in the country of their origin. They identify with Jesus in their desire to see people saved, healed and delivered. Salvation is accepting Jesus as Saviour; healing of body, soul and spirit is promised by Jesus; deliverance is complete freedom from any addiction. Often, they will relate to the passage of scripture that follows:

Romans 10: 13 For, "Everyone who calls on the name of the Lord shall be saved."[f]

14 How then shall they call on Him in whom they have not believed? And how shall they believe in Him of whom they have not heard? And how shall they hear without a preacher? 15 And how shall they preach unless they are sent? As it is written: "How beautiful are the feet of those who preach the gospel of peace, who bring good news of good things!"[g]

They identify that they can do it. Something within their heart compels them to go preach the gospel at any opportunity. Several of the Evangelists I have mentioned from this past century have had a supernatural healing or deliverance and they use their testimony to inspire faith in others. Their words are with authority because they have known that God could save them. Many of them know if God could save them, God could save anyone.

Hebrews 7: 25 Therefore He is able to save to the uttermost those who come to God through Him, because He at all times lives to make intercession for them.

The Evangelist is mostly concerned with this very moment and those who don't know Jesus Christ who could die and spend eternity in hell. Often in their messages, they will ask the question if the crowd is certain of their destiny. A true Christian knows that he or she is right with God and will live forever. Those in sin, may repent and rededicate their lives. A sinner who is caught in a lifestyle of sin and addiction hears the good news that they don't have to be ensnared by evil or by any type of addiction, get hope believing that God will certainly set them free. What happens is as the Evangelist preaches, he or she will use scriptures that inspire faith in the people who are listening.

Christian Media

Christian Media is once more an excellent way to reach people. I have heard testimonies of people that are amazing. For instance, at the moment the person who was addicted to sins and illegal activity, turned on the TV, the message spoke directly to him as if God was speaking through the preacher. I do believe God uses Christian Media for evangelism. In some countries where worshipping as a Christian is forbidden, people use their satellite dishes to get Christian teaching. The thing that most interests them is healing and miracles. If they hear or see such proof of healing and miracles as can been seen in most Evangelistic meetings, they will secretly become Christians.

Travel

I have not known of too many evangelists who do not travel. Part of their call is to go from place to place preaching about Jesus. In Africa, there are sometimes gatherings of a million people in these crusades. People walk for days to attend them, bringing the sick with faith for a miracle. There are some Evangelists that have special anointings. What I mean by that is there are certain giftings that are unusual about them that maybe no other person has. For instance, Oral Roberts had a sign from God that his hand would tingle and burn and he would know how many demons to cast out and what they were. Kathryn Kulman would speak, and at her word, people would be slain in the spirit. Benny Hinn also has been used with healings and miracles. Often as the people are worshipping in his crusade meetings, people are healed by simply worshipping God. I have seen him with boldness cast our demons. I have seen people set free from physical disease and addictions because of his preaching and teaching.

God anoints the Evangelism with wording that is exact, precise and like a sharp sword that pierces the hearts of the people. Rod Parsley for instance may preach about salvation, healing and deliverance of Jesus Christ and all of the church will receive something from God. Sometimes the pastor has a strong evangelist calling such as Rod Parsley but usually evangelists are not pastors unless they are the missionary pastors or responsible for gathering people and training people for missions and evangelism.

The Call

An evangelist first gets the calling sure in his or her heart. Next, they are either groomed by senior ministers or adopted by other evangelists to travel together. An example is that Kenneth Copeland flew Oral Roberts to meetings and prayed for people before he was in released in full time ministry. He did learn by seeing the lifestyle and heart of an Evangelist. Jerry Savelle travelled with Kenneth Copeland often preaching to people on the streets in between the services. Lester Summerall met Smith Wiggelsworth and shared with him and learned of him and was mentored by him and anointed by him for service. I have seen Lester Summarall pray over and pour into Rod Parsley prophesying over them imparting a transference anointing.

My main point is God has got to mentor you. The only way to learn to be an effective evangelist is to do it and to see effective evangelists and learn from them. I believe it is a principle of the kingdom for all ministry gifts. God wants the experienced to train up and mentor the generations to come. I have been eye witness to impartation meetings where one older minister prays and imparts an anointing on the younger one. It is a transference of anointing.

The Lifestyle

Most evangelists are pretty radical people in lifestyle. They think about

Jesus; they talk about Jesus; they labour winning souls for Jesus; they care about the souls of people like Jesus. Their family lives often involve family missions and ministry together. Certainly, it matters that the spouse be given to evangelism and ministry. If not, they cannot remain together, The Evangelists I know of never stop. They labour until God takes them from the earth. I witnessed Lester Sumerall in his 80's preaching and evangelizing and training up new ministers who found it tough to keep up with him.

It is essential that an Evangelist remain pure. Mary Alice Isleib coined this phrase but it so good I am using it "The purity of the gospel is the power of the gospel." In other words if the message is not pure, it has no value. The messenger of the gospel must remain sexually pure; not be given to pride or covetousness. The person should partner with strong people of faith and holiness who will keep the gospel the main thing always. It should never become a side thing, It is the main reason we sing and worship. It is the main reason we are compelled to give financially so people can be fed and clothed and given schooling.

Jesus is the main reason. This must be the vision purpose statement – to help others come to know Jesus. God can speak to you about other aspects of your ministry. For instance, there are athletes for Christ; there are singers and concerts for Christ. The Onething Conference in Kansas and the Passion Conference in Atlanta are huge events where thousands (Usually 20, 000 or more) of youth get to learn about Christ. There is excellent worship and praise. There is excitement and joy in meeting so many new people. Jesus is the main thing in these events.

At the start of the 20th century, there was a release of Evangelists. Also in the 19050's there were many evangelists. Some of them are still preaching and teaching today. It is more rare now to see Evangelistic crusades in North America. Greg Laurie, last year had a meeting with about 100, 000 people gathered to hear an evangelistic message in the USA. There have not been many who gather people in North America for salvation for the last several decades. Part of the reason is in the 1970's there was a movement in the body of Christ for Teachers of the Word. They were well studied, some very educated people who taught the doctrines of Christ, the foundations and also various aspects of Christian life to their churches. Strong teaching ministries were on Christian TV teaching God's word.

In the 1980's and 1990's there was a strong Prophetic and Apostolic Move of God in North America. It still continues today. It involves teaching the people, releasing them in giftings of the Holy Spirit and commissioning them in ministry. I do believe that we need evangelists in the present day more than ever before. It is not that the Church can't do something. There are outreaches. All members of the body of Christ are called to win souls. There are spurts of efforts by people. I thank God for them. I truly believe we need a move of Evangelism like we have never seen in the past.

Angel with sword

I often pray regarding the next year to seek the LORD for a word that would inspire me and guide me for the new year. I don't know how it came but it most certainly came to me this past year. There is an angel who will sing his sword over the earth and release the everlasting gospel in a new dimension such as has never been before. It is a sword of Evangelism.

Revelation 14: 6 Then I saw another angel flying in the midst of heaven, having the eternal gospel to preach to those who dwell on the earth, to every nation and tribe and tongue and people. 7 He said with a loud voice, "Fear God and give Him glory, for the hour of His judgment has come. Worship Him who made heaven and earth, the sea and the springs of water."

I am believing God and praying for a release of that angel and the gospel to be released NSEW throughout the earth. Surely, it is a sign of God's return. Jesus Christ will not return until all nations receive the gospel message. It is of most importance that those who are evangelists train up and mentor those who feel a call for evangelism. It is essential that we train up and fortify our frontline evangelists and missionaries so that they may receive the best possible training. We as the church of North America (I believe that North America funds most of the missionary outreach in the world) emphasize evangelism.

Matthew 24: 14 And this gospel of the kingdom will be preached throughout the world as a testimony to all nations, and then the end will come.

I remember when I walked in my home town and was usually given a tract or told about Jesus by somebody most certainly. No more do those people do it. I don't know why. I do know there have been so many changes in the Body of Christ that the emphasis has been on body ministry. I believe in it. I am praying that God will release the evangelists who will be passionate for souls and for sharing Christ with as many people as possible. You may be that person that has a miraculous testimony of how God set you free from addictions. Maybe you have a good job and a good income.

I pray God will touch your heart with the truth that your miraculous deliverance is not something that should be kept a secret. They will only know about it if you share with others.

Maybe you start an evangelistic group in your church. You would pray together and go door to door. You could rent a space in a public park to share Christian music and bring a gospel message. Maybe you would go on a mission's trip. I don't know how God may direct you. If you know that this chapter has touched your heart and you feel that you have a calling to share Christ with people, please don't let it go as though it is nothing. God created you. God saved you. God can use you. You certainly can post scriptures to social media and advertise any outreaches that your church does that way. You could start a Christian Blog.

Isaiah 49: 2 He has made my mouth like a sharp sword;
    in the shadow of His hand He has hidden me
and made me a select arrow;

Commitment

Your prayer of commitment is the first step. Next, start sowing financially into existing well renown evangelists who are preaching the gospel. Learn all you can from the, Pray that God will give you a mentor or friend to evangelize with. It's always easier with a friend or a small group.

Strategy

Begin to strategize. Get passionate and commit yourself to Christ that you could use your resources, skills and efforts to help in evangelism in some way. You may not leave your secular job. God can use you with those skills and with your education and training to reach others. Even if you can't publically pray for people in your job, you could privately pray for people in your job. Pray that God can lead you to people who can help you with your calling. Pray for people where God can use you with your calling.

Some large ministries who may come near you always need local people to help serve, take an offering, seat people etc. Should you get the chance, volunteer. You don't know where that first effort will lead you. Sometimes large Christian associations recruit people who can help them. For instance, Marilyn Hickey always invites and trains her partners to go with her on missionary trips. The people are taught how to pray for others and lead them to Christ. It would be an excellent opportunity.

The First Evangelist

The first evangelist was a woman. She was the woman of Samaria. Jesus speaks with her there at the well in Samaria. He a Jew, broke all custom and spoke with a woman a known enemy of the Jew. He revealed the secrets of her heart, She knows that only God knows the things about her that Jesus speaks openly with her about, and immediately asks him about worship.

John 4: 21 Jesus said to her, "Woman, believe Me, the hour is coming when neither on this mountain nor in Jerusalem will you worship the Father. 22 You worship what you do not know; we know what we worship, for salvation is of the Jews. 23 Yet the hour is coming, and is now here, when the true worshippers will worship the Father in spirit and truth. For the Father seeks such to worship Him. 24 God is Spirit, and those who worship Him must worship Him in spirit and truth."

The woman, an adulterer, someone most people would distain, confesses she believes Messiah will come. Jesus reveals himself to her as Messiah.

John 4: 25 The woman said to Him, "I know that Messiah is coming" (who is called Christ). "When He comes, He will tell us all things."

26 Jesus said to her, "I who speak to you am He."

Immediately she receives the truth. She leaves her water pot and runs into town sharing that certainly she has met the Messiah. Please see, normally a woman who is living a sinful life doesn't run through the streets talking about the Messiah. Something happened at the well that day. She believed that Jesus is Messiah because of his words of wisdom about her and his discerning of spirits.

Philip the Evangelist

Philip the evangelist is preaching in Samaria and there is a mighty move of God. It could be compared to any successful gospel campaign. There he shared the word and many people believed. Most preachers who were having successful meetings wouldn't leave to go elsewhere.

Acts 8: 4 Therefore those who were scattered went everywhere preaching the word. 5 Philip went down to the city of Samaria and preached Christ to them. 6 When the crowds heard Philip and saw the miracles which he did, they listened in unity to what he said. 7 For unclean spirits, crying with a loud voice, came out of many who were possessed. And many who were paralyzed or lame were healed. 8 So there was much joy in that city.

God cared about others also. In the midst of a successful preaching campaign the angel of the LORD instructs Philip to leave and to go to a certain place. Philip obeyed. Notice that his emphasis wasn't on what he had done or the success of the moment. He was God's servant and he obeyed. He saw one man, an Ethiopian Eunuch, reading scripture and at the exact spot that he was reading about the Messiah he could not comprehend it. He asks Philip if he knows what it is. The opportunity is a God ordained moment. God prepared that Eunuch to be desiring to know about God and Philip obeyed and was there to help.

Acts 8: 26 Now an angel of the Lord said to Philip, "Rise up and go toward the south on the way that goes down from Jerusalem to Gaza." This is desert. 27 So he rose up and went. And there was a man of Ethiopia, a eunuch of great authority under Candace, queen of the Ethiopians, who was in command of her entire treasury. He had come to Jerusalem to worship. 28 He was returning, sitting in his chariot and reading the book of Isaiah the prophet. 29 The Spirit said to Philip, "Go to this chariot and stay with it."
30 Then Philip ran to him, and heard him read the book of Isaiah the prophet, and said, "Do you understand what you are reading?"

31 He said, "How can I, unless someone guides me?" So he invited Philip to come up and sit with him.

At the exact spot in Isaiah 53 where Messiah gives his life as a ransom, Philip preaches Jesus Christ to him. The Eunuch is completely believing and accepts the gospel coming from Philip. The Eunuch wants to be baptized. They stop the caravan and Philip baptizes the Ethiopian who will bring the gospel to his country. Immediately, Philip is translated. That is the Spirit of God carries him to a different place. If Philip had not obeyed, perhaps Ethiopia would not have received the gospel for many more years. An evangelist must be discerning and obedient to the Holy Spirit.

Evangelists should have the doctrines of Christ clearly. I was saved one day, I started evangelizing, I didn't even know what to do, but I knew I had met Jesus, so I brought the person to mature Christian who could pray with her to receive Christ. Evangelists should try to get the people some type of association with churches in that person's home town. It is essential that a new Christian come to know the doctrines and foundations of the faith. Evangelists should team up with churches in large crusades so people could find a church home.

Evangelists may travel constantly but they should team up with churches. I've known of some evangelists who have stayed on with successful meetings and there were revivals such as in Brownsville and Toronto in the 1990's. Jentzen Franklin was an Evangelist who was scheduled to preach at a Church a year in advance and when he got there, he preached a funeral service for the pastor who had died. The congregation begged him to stay and be their pastor and he did. Free Chapel is known for its missions outreaches and evangelistic outreaches as well as its excellence in teaching the word of God.

Evangelists care for thousands of people coming to Christ but with the same passion for Christ he or she will preach to one soul. You may be an evangelist that may preach to crowd or perhaps you will preach one on one with people. Both are necessary. Evangelists has a heart for the people to see them saved, healed and set free from addictions. Keep your heart humble and let God use you. Keep Jesus as the main thing.

Chapter end questions

1. Write the names of 2 or 3 evangelists that you know of who have made a difference in North America.
2. Consider yourself and evangelism. Is it something you can do easily or is it something that is tough for you and why?
3. Consider ways for yourself and imagine doing it, volunteering your church to evangelize.
4. Consider some way you could help to finance the evangelists you know of who are preaching Jesus Christ throughout the world.

5 PASTORS

Pastors

Ephesians 4: 11 He gave some to be apostles, prophets, evangelists, pastors, and teachers, 12 for the equipping of the saints, for the work of service, and for the building up of the body of Christ,

Using the word ministry usually makes people think about pastors. Some people don't know any of the other five-fold ministry. Pastors are leaders in the church. They have a strong desire to shepherd or organize and care for God's people. They are able to see or envision an event or an opportunity for God's people and choose people who are gifted to help him or her and organize all aspects of it so it is accomplished. They are leaders; that means others acknowledge that truly the person has a gift to lead. The person's ideas inspire and enable others to serve God and contribute their gifts and talents. The calling of God as a Pastor is usually a lifelong call to a particular congregation. Usually, pastors don't move from church to church frequently. A good sign the pastor is with the right congregation is the length of ministry with them. Usually, people are given progressive roles as a pastor. That is one may over sea youth and later be assigned assistant pastor role. Rarely does a man or woman become senior pastor immediately in a denominational church.

There all different types of pastors in large churches. I mean churches upwards of a 1000 people. For instance, one pastor may be devoted to missions; a different pastor may oversee Spiritual gifts etc. In most small churches (20 – 100 people) pastors are the preachers who bring the word of God to the people. I have assisted in ministry in smaller churches by volunteering to teach. I have been in large churches mainly and enjoyed my experience thoroughly because of the variety of offerings of courses, experience, activity and serving opportunities. Smaller churches usually do not have as many such opportunities. I have also attended churches of approximal 200 people. I would term these churches mid-size churches. Often there are several pastors or elders and deacons who offer classes and opportunities for spiritual growth. All pastors have some common aspects. They love people; they care about the sheep's spiritual growth; they desire to share God's word to build up and encourage people. I believe most pastors are also encouragers as they share God's word as the standard for our lives.

Criteria for ministry

The scriptures are pretty strict on requirements for ministry. The person must live a lifestyle of excellence This includes the following list.

1 Timothy 3: 3 This is a faithful saying: If a man desires the office of an overseer, he desires a good work. 2 An overseer then must be blameless, the husband of one wife, sober, self-controlled, respectable, hospitable, able to teach; 3 not given to drunkenness, not violent, not greedy for money, but patient, not argumentative, not covetous; 4 and one who manages his own house well, having his children in submission with all reverence.

8 Likewise deacons must be serious, not insincere, not given to much wine, not greedy, 9 keeping the mystery of the faith in a pure conscience. 10 And let them first be tested; then, being found blameless, let them serve as deacons.

11 Likewise, their wives must be serious, not slanderers, sober, and faithful in all things.

12 Let the deacons be the husbands of one wife, managing their children and their own houses well. 13 For those who have served well in the office of deacon purchase for themselves good standing and great boldness in the faith, which is in Christ Jesus.

Blameless means they do not have any ongoing character fault that causes people to say negative things about them. Some churches literally apply the scripture that a pastor cannot divorce and remarry. Sober has to do both with self-control concerning alcohol but also someone who is serious about ministry. Respected by the church members, these people should also be respected from those who are not church members; for example, in a secular job. Hospitality and loved of people go together. The pastors must enjoy gatherings of people and see that those gatherings are excellent. This could include opening their homes to people, but it could also be gathering people in other buildings including restaurants and other public places or others' homes.

Teaching God's word is a requirement as that is usually the main job of a pastor. The pastors must love God's word and desire to share God's word with others. It is the analogy of a shepherd and his or her sheep. All of these aspects are related to character and personal traits. Please notice it. Scripture does not list a group of spiritual gifts the pastors must have or levels of anointing they have, or any other requirements of gifting besides able to teach. I have listed the criteria for deacons here as deacons are servants in the church and they are also in leadership roles. Some churches promote deacons to elders and they are appointed opportunities to share God's word with the people.

How a pastor knows he or she is called into ministry

I have known children who love God's word completely and thoroughly and dig into God's word for themselves and want to talk about God's word with others. They knew they wanted to be pastors in grade 4 or 5 of elementary school. I have known others who are mostly servants in the church, faithful, diligent and trustworthy who feel a tugging at their hearts for ministry training in their adult years. I attended churches where women were the senior pastors. Unfortunately, there is still prejudice about women in ministry in many churches.

Galatians 3: 27 For as many of you as have been baptized into Christ have put on Christ. 28 There is neither Jew nor Greek, there is neither slave nor free, and there is neither male nor female, for you are all one in Christ Jesus. 29 If you are Christ's, then you are Abraham's seed, and heirs according to the promise.

Some people have a God ordained supernatural experience that changes their life direction and cause them to want to be pastors. Others simply feel an inner witness or tug at their hearts in that direction. God can confirm the calling. Using peace as an umpire (Gloria Copeland), a person may say aloud to God in prayer, " I am believing I am going to study for ministry" talking to God and ask God to either confirm it to you or correct you if it is not what you should be doing. I truly believe this simple but effective technique of speaking with God and letting Him confirm things or steer you in a different direction is necessary for all types of ministry.

True pastors never choose the job because it has good perks or pay, or is a nice thing to do. If a person only chooses becoming a pastor for any reason except caring for God's people, he or she will hate his or her job and or be an ineffective communicator for Christ. The scripture makes it clear that a shepherd will lead by his voice. What that means is that the sheep will gather at the voice of the true shepherd. There will be people who want to hear the person preach or teach.

The Voice

John 10: 2 But he who enters by the door is the shepherd of the sheep. 3

To him the doorkeeper opens, and the sheep hear his voice. He calls his own sheep by name, and he leads them out. 4 When he brings out his own sheep, he goes before them. And the sheep follow him, for they know his voice

An example of this for those people not raised in the country with sheep, is that your pets respond to your voice. The animals recognize the voice, also the love you have shown towards them. Some animals gather to someone who is calling them. Some animals run from some people that are calling them.

John 10: 5 Yet they will never follow a stranger, but will run away from him. For they do not know the voice of strangers."

The Voice brings peace

Animals can sense a person's intents much like children do. Sheep that follow a shepherd are usually congregations of people. The main reasons for attending a church should be connected with the pastors and the word of God that is taught at that church. Once Christians find a place that God has for them, they will feel as comfortable as though they are home. They will receive instruction, correction, encouragement etc. from the pastor or pastors. If that does not happen, the person is not in the right place.

I can remember on several occasions being in a church that I would attend. The first day, I could sense that I belonged by the pastor's words and message. I felt an inner witness (peace) that it was the right place for me to stay. There are many reasons that people choose churches and attend churches. I am discussing only the scriptural proofs of why people choose certain places because of the voice of the shepherd.

Feeding the Sheep

The feeding of the sheep involves preparing a message or series of messages for God's people because the pastor senses spiritually it is what the people need. In the large churches I attended, the pastor not only prepared the sermon but prayed and ask God to reveal to him what the sheep needed and received divine confirmation and sometimes scriptures or direct words to speak. I would call that type of preaching prophetic preaching. Prophetic preaching is God gives the scriptures and the direction to the pastor rather than the pastor determining what to do. I have learned that both exist – the pastor preparing what he or believes the people need and God revealing to the pastor what to speak on. They are not the same at all. Their impact is not the same. However, I would not say that a pastor who prayerfully plans a sermon is ineffective. Most certainly he or she is reaching some people. Many congregations will be used to this and they often don't know any other way.

A preacher who is prophetic in gifting who hears God's voice directing him or her with scriptures and direction to speak to the people is not so common. The preaching is dynamic and it as though every single word the person speaks it directly aimed at your spirit. In those types of preaching services, the people receive not only encouragement but a direct stimulation of their faith causing them to be built up and strengthened and their faith to arise. Often, miracles, healings and rededication of people to God occur in those types of meetings. That was the only type of church I knew for the first 15 or 16 years of my Christian life. The shepherds heard God's voice and spoke it to the people. I would compare it much like Moses hearing from God directly and speaking it to the people of Israel throughout the books of Exodus and Deuteronomy.

A preacher who is preaching prophetically will be serving a special meal for the sheep: the mature Christians will be getting steak from the Word; they can grow from it; carnal Christians will feel a tug at their hearts and rededicate their lives to God; new Christians will learn some of the truths of God so they can become mature Christians. New Christians must learn the doctrines of Christ. I know it is sometimes taught separately in classes but it can also and should also be mentioned in sermons as God leads.

There should be teaching and practice of the sacraments in the local church. Water Baptism, the LORD's supper and other such things must be taught. There are some people who come to the church not knowing any of these things. If we do not teach them, they will not know. The pastor must also reach the majority of the congregation with "nuggets'" it is a term my friend uses to talk about the truths that God can reveal to a Christian even though he or she knows the scriptures – they are special scriptures of revelation God can bring to a person. It is literally like panning for gold and finding gold nuggets in with the sand. These nuggets will prompt a Christian to do further study and often to take action doing something for God. It may mean teaching a class or serving in an outreach or special giving etc.

There are books that a pastor can buy with prepared sermons in it. He or she would get the scriptures and the message from the book. This is used by some. It is not highly regarded by myself. I consider this technique to be compared to a TV dinner. I like TV dinners. If there is no other option, I choose it. It is not my first choice. TV dinners have a portion of sliced meat, a dab of vegetable and a dab of dessert. You most certainly won't be getting your ½ cup portion of fruit and vegetables from it. It often has preservative in it with a huge list of chemicals used to keep it fresh. Packaged sermons can never replace a real prayerful pastor who considers what to give the people. It is totally the opposite of a prophetic preacher who hears from God and speaks the word.

Pastors are ultimately responsible for all the sheep in their care. That includes those who preach from the prepackaged sermons or those who get a word from God directly. If these pastors had influence in your life, they will give account for it. That is they must be faithful to do all they can to help you grown spiritually. A word that reaches the majority of the people to give them encouragement, comfort and direction, with special nuggets for the mature Christians and "milk" for the new Christians (1 Peter 2:2), cannot be designed by a person. It is too complex for someone to do. Only God can inspire a person to reach all these different kinds of people. God can do it. After an anointed word, a word that does all of the above list, there is usually a response by the people.

I've been in services where there isn't even an altar call but the people come forward kneeling in prayer. Some lie prostrate on the ground. The people know that God is using the minster to reach them. They respond to God by giving their lives in a new way. I did not know there were churches that didn't culminate the service with an altar call. An altar call is an opportunity for the congregation to respond to the word of God that was preached by praying. In my own life, these opportunities have transformed my life completely.

The first church I attended had a literal wooden alar – a place to kneel. It makes it easier for the person praying because he or she can kneel against the wood. Also, the altar worker can pray with you by standing on the other side of the wooden rail. It is something rare or non-existent in most Pentecostal or charismatic churches. I don't believe it is a good thing. Giving the people a place to worship and pray – that is consecrated for such a purpose somehow makes it easier for the altar call. It becomes the focus at the end of a service. People gather there to give themselves to God. It also discourages people from talking or jesting at the altar. They go to other areas within the church to chat. The altar is a place of prayer.

Sermons and other responsibilities

The sermons themselves are only part of what a pastor does. It is an important part. In some small congregations, the pastor is the janitor and repairman. In some small churches, the pastor is the only one who does visitation in home. The pastor deals with those who want to marry or want to divorce etc. I have not seen very many small congregations where the pastor is assisted by many people in different roles of the church and I am not sure on the reason. I mean I'm not sure that there is not some reason the church never grows beyond 40 people.

I am not against small churches; If more people were involved in helping the pastor, they could accomplish much more. Size is not the only determiner of a successful church. There may be large churches where the church is led astray by a wolf in sheep's clothing. Please see I am talking about the principle of God using a pastor with other people to effectively be a body of Christ in a place. The normal Christian church should be growing in size and in maturity of believers and in Godly character as well as outreach and missions. All of these things are the pastor's responsibility to pray about.

Church Growth

A healthy church is growing. In the church I currently go to, there isn't a Sunday that there are not visitors to the church. Not all of the people who come to Church are Christians. The pastor has got to find ways to reaching those non-believers who are interested in God as well as the congregation as well as outreach ministries etc.

I have known excellent pastors who are in large churches who train other pastors and give progressive responsibilities to potential leaders. They don't do all the visitation, but they do some. They don't do the janitorial but sometimes they hold church cleaning days and work alongside of all the people. Good pastors stay involved with the sheep no matter how large the church gets. A good shepherd in a large church who keeps investing in potential leaders and mentoring them to become pastors and launching new churches and sending teams to do it often has an Apostolic gifting. I have known of large churches who have literally multiplied and have released many pastoral teams to start churches throughout North America and the world. A good shepherd is one who gives his or her life for the sheep.

John 10: 11 "I am the good shepherd. The good shepherd lays down His life for the sheep. 12 But he who is a hired hand, and not a shepherd, who does not own the sheep, sees the wolf coming, and leaves the sheep, and runs away. So the wolf catches the sheep and scatters them. 13 The hired hand runs away because he is a hired hand and does not care about the sheep.

Caring for the Sheep

There is a covering aspect or oversight protection of the sheep that is true to all true pastors. They are loyal to the sheep and do whatever they can to care for the sheep. I have heard of excellent preachers explain that sheep are a good analogy for people because sheep are not especially bright animals. They may wander off and get caught in some bush; they may get into bramble weeds or pickers. They are followers. If one sheep is lost and it is the predominant sheep, all of the other sheep will get lost with it. A good shepherd will care for all of the sheep. That means he or she knows the things going on in the church. In large churches, it means communicating regularly with all the pastors and their concerns. It means knowing if someone is missing.

I had a pastor, Guillermo, it was in a church of about 200, who would phone you personally if you missed more than one service. He wasn't trying to bother you. He truly cared about the sheep and would check up on them personally to see if you needed anything. That same pastor knew of a youth who was saved and set free from addictions. The youth was a new Christian and was the only Christian in his family. He would stop coming to church and go back to his old lifestyle. My pastor would go to his home, speak with him, get him to repent from falling away and literally bring him to church. I have witnessed my pastor disciple several youths in this manner. What he would do is involve them in maintenance roles in the church and get them to help serve in within the church atmosphere during the week (the youth had dropped out of school) so most of their days were spent with godly people. He would invite them into his home and include them in youth events. It gave them a different point of view and helped them to stay clean.

Luke 15: 3 So He told them this parable, saying, 4 "What man among you having a hundred sheep and losing one of them does not leave the ninety-nine in the wilderness and go after the one which is lost until he finds it? 5 And when he has found it, he places it on his shoulders, rejoicing. 6 Then when he comes home, he calls together his friends and neighbors, saying to them, 'Rejoice with me, for I have found my sheep which was lost.

Christian Media Shepherds

It is not a good indication if there are many people in the church who receive no spiritual food from the service. That means the pastor may bring a word that is nice but doesn't get to you spiritually at all. I myself know what it is like to rely on Christian media for spiritual food. There is excellent teaching and preaching from apostles, prophets, evangelists, teachers and missionaries that is available 24/9 because of the miracle of Christian media. I thank God for it. Because I was not raised in a Christian home, I often used Christian media to be my Christian support. For the past several years I have relied on it strongly for spiritual food. I Had the Glory Star, Christian satellite network with close to 70 stations – all Christian. It was excellent and it is excellent. It is not the same as being in person in a service but it can feed you spiritually in the same way. What isn't there is opportunities to meet people, encourage people, volunteer or use your spiritual gifts in the church. All of those things are really important. I believe it is God's will to have all Christians in a place where they can be fed spiritually as well as contribute.

Often, I thought I was the only one in this situation. There are many on line churches rising up and churches that stream their services over the Internet because of people who cannot get to church for one reason or another. Although I know it isn't the best that could be (because I have known belonging in a church) Internet and satellite options have kept me refreshed and well – rounded as well as built me up spiritually and given me truths and teaching that I could never get locally. I don't know where the realm of on line churches will go. There are thousands of people in North America who rely on Christian Media rather than a local church to nourish them. I do believe it is God's will for people to gather together; although it is excellent and I thank God for Christian media, it doesn't replace totally the experience of being a part pf the congregation and using the gifts of the Spirit to prophesy or speak in tongues or interpret tongues etc.

Giving

A spiritual principle is to give to the storehouse or the place where you receive spiritual food. It is almost always the local church. I have known this to be true for many years of my Christian life. I also know what it is like to receive most of my spiritual encouragement and spiritual food from Christian media. In some of these situations it is necessary – not because of any religious rule but because of the following principle: give to the place that feeds you.

1 Corinthians 9: 11 If we have sown for you spiritual things, is it a great thing if we shall reap your material things? 12 If others partake of this right over you, should not we instead?

Nevertheless, we have not used this right, but suffer all things, lest we might hinder the gospel of Christ.

13 Do you not know that those who minister unto holy things live from the things of the temple? And do you not know that those who wait at the altar partake of the altar? 14 In the same way, the Lord has ordained that those who preach the gospel should live from the gospel.

Prayer protection

A true shepherd will also be praying for his or her congregation. There would be a sense of caring as though the people are a family. The shepherd would pray for the sheep not only in the service or in visitations but as a part of his or her own private prayer life. The people will also pray for their pastors. As the pastors are praying for their sheep, God can quicken a person or family to the pastor and perhaps prompt him or her to contact the person or family. Such a thing has occurred in my life where the Pastor phoned me and felt strongly to assign me a position of leadership. I felt overwhelmed at first because I know it had to be God doing it.

The pastor and pastors are a spiritual covering over the people. Just as a shepherd would fight against any enemy of the sheep, wolves or bears, a pastor will be quickened in prayer for his or her sheep. If the congregation is praying for the pastors, it releases angels to protect and guard them. Apostles and or bishops are the covering for a local Church. They should add spiritual value to the pastors and ministry team as well as care for them to encourage them and strengthen them as leaders.

Ministry Routines

Other duties of a pastor include teaching Bible classes. The pastors in a large church usually have appointed main duties. It doesn't mean they never minster from the pulpit. Sometimes they do, but mostly they teach classes, visit people, do funerals or weddings, baptisms, etc. In a smaller church, it is necessary for the pastor and elders and deacons to function together to cover all the aspects of ministry including all the classes ad duties listed above.

What I enjoy in a large church is that there be an offering of so many classes a person cannot attend them all. The church should not only be for Sundays and a mid-week service but it should be used by the people every day. In large churches especially, the church is a gathering place for all type of reasons. There are Bible classes. There are sports teams; there are discipling groups; there are lectures on how to prepare for a job or write a resume; there are knitting groups or various ages group gatherings.

Please see it is possible that the youth could be playing volleyball in the gym while the men are meeting in the sanctuary while some are volunteering to packages boxes for a food bank. I believe the more activities offered, can give people a gathering place for ministry themselves. Remember the reason the ministry gifts are given to the Church is to build up, strengthen, equip the saints to minister in their own giftings. The ministry team does the equipping. The church members get involved in aspects of ministry.

Ephesians 4: 12 for the equipping of the saints, for the work of service, and for the building up of the body of Christ, 13 until we all come into the unity of the faith and of the knowledge of the Son of God, into a complete man, to the measure of the stature of the fullness of Christ,

A sign of a healthy church is the number of volunteers and people active in volunteer ministry. This includes visitation, outreach, prayer, evangelistic programs, special events etc. The more people who are functioning and giving in ministry, directly shows they are well nourished. The sheep will want to use their spiritual gifts and the result will be most people being involved in some aspect of church life and ministry.

The pastor is not Omnipresent

It is not right for a congregation of any size to expect the pastor or pastors to do everything. For example, even if the large church has nine pastors, they cannot personally handle the 1,500 people in every area of their lives. Church is not something we go to. We are the Church; we gather in a building. Usually, it is the elders and deacons who volunteer to do some of the other classes or activities but there could also be leaders who are mature Christians that teach and minister in the church in various roles. The people will love what they do; they will support the ministry team. They will help to build up the church.

I have volunteered in some small churches that I did not regularly attend. I knew there was a specific need for a teacher and I volunteered. Mostly it was for Vacation Bible school. I also was recruited by my friends who started a church to help with the youth. It was my pleasure to serve the body of Christ in this way. I believed it was important and God tugged at my heart to volunteer. I don't regret one minute of it. I did notice in those smaller churches, the expectations of the pastor were demanding. The only way for small churches to do all that would make a small church healthy would be for more people to get involved in different aspects so that perhaps a mature Christian could teach a class on one night. The youth could gather on a different day. The women would get together a different day etc. I am saying lay people should consider their spiritual gifts as important to use in the church and to help the pastor or pastors.

Pastors must train up leaders

Ministry is a lifelong call but the ministers should also have a private life. The pastors should be able to be with their families without interruption. The pastors should be able to take a day off knowing that somebody who is trained is going to preach and conduct the service with excellence. It is important in a church of any size to train up leaders within the church to assist and become a part of the ministry team – whether paid or volunteer.

I have been in churches where there have been leadership training classes. The pastor or one of the pastors would teach it. It gave both preaching and teaching and a practical aspect of ministry training. What the result was that the church grew and more and more ministry aspects were added to the church because more people with different talents became involved. There is a gym; a place for youth to play; more than one campus; an arts and dance and creative writing aspect of worship taught; there is a Christian school; there are family movie nights at the church; there are events and Bible classes for all types of people. The fruit of abundance is upon that place because of the training of leaders and the release of leaders to participate in equipping the saints.

Lifestyle

The pastors and their families are to live as examples in the church. All those who are in leadership in a church must give account for their areas of responsibility. Scripture explains that leaders are held to a strict standard. Because leaders have more authority, they will give account for more.

James 3: 1 My brothers, not many of you should become teachers, knowing that we shall receive the greater judgment.

People within the church should see godly character expressed through the pastors. The pastors should be well respected in the community. Even non-Christians should be able to say something positive about the Christian leaders. How a Christian leader lives his or her life is important because so many people are influenced by them. A Christian leader who fails morally – who sins – does much damage to many people. If the sin includes sexual immorality, what happens is the other person is damaged in a terrible way as a trust was violated. The congregation will scatter. People sometimes wander from place to place not finding a place of belonging. They get ensnared in sins and in a lifestyle they were once protected from by their spiritual covering. I have seen and been a part of congregations where such horrible things occurred. Years later, my constant care for the wandering sheep is in my prayers. Mostly, I pray that God would gather them and give them places of peace. I do pray God would grant them repentance.

I do believe in restoration of pastors. The scripture teaches it. I have read of successful restorations of people in ministry.

Galatians 6: 1 Brothers, if a man is caught in any transgression, you who are spiritual should restore such a one in the spirit of meekness, watching yourselves, lest you also be tempted.

The way of God's word teaches restoration. A minister who willfully sins must confess it before his or her congregation and with other authorities witnessing it. Usually, the person is removed from ministry responsibility for a duration.

Please know a minister who has gifts from God will not lose the gifts if they sin. God never revokes his gifts. He has gifts and charisma and he is doing something for God by teaching and preaching. I believe in God's forgiveness. I do believe in restoration. I do believe it must be prefaced by repentance.

The primary temptations that come to ministers are sexual sin, covetousness and pride. They are traps that the devil can use to ensnare a pastor or a minister of any type.

1 John 2: 16 For all that is in the world—the lust of the flesh, the lust of the eyes, and the pride of life—is not of the Father, but is of the world. 17 The world and its desires are passing away, but the one who does the will of God lives forever.

I believe there are safeguards that should be a part of each leader's life: the Billy Graham method of dealing with people of the opposite sex is rather strict but it is excellent– that is only be with members of the opposite sex in the presence of your spouse or with a colleague. The only way to avoid pride is to purpose in your heart to give God all the glory and to take part in all types of ministry. I do believe the sacrament of foot washing helps to eliminate pride.

Close friendships with strong Christians is important: Accountability. Prayer with the spouse and including the spouse in as many possible activities are also good. I have successfully seen husbands and wives in ministry together. They both have responsibilities in the church and as a team they lead the people. I have seen many married people who are co pastors that are successful in ministry.

Ideal Ministry Team

I believe it would be God's ideal for the five-fold ministry to be in each church. Together they are as fingers on a hand. They work most effectively together. One by itself can do something but together all of them have a strong potential to accomplish something. A way of doing it if it does not exist in your local church is to welcome visiting ministers at least several times a year. I would do it at least once a month. What happens is the church grows in a more dynamic way. There is constant nourishing for all types of people by Apostles, Prophets, Pastors, Teachers and Evangelists. I believe the Antioch Church had it (Acts 11).

The five-fold ministry in the church will mean that missions teams are constantly being sent out; it will mean there is care for the widows and orphans; it will mean there is excellent preaching and teaching; it will mean the people will be moved to give financially to other ministries and churches. It will mean the full functioning of the church as a Church body. Ministers should see the need for and want the five-fold ministry in their lives and in their churches. They should not see the other minister as competition but as a compliment to themselves.

Overseer of the Church

The successful church will have a balance of teaching from the various five-fold ministry. There will be prophetic messages and prophetic ministry. There will be Apostolic commissioning and preaching. There will be evangelism and evangelistic outreach. There will be pastoral care for the needs of the local church including prayer, services, sacraments, marriage, burial, giving to the widows and orphans etc. There will be strong teaching of God's word. A church with these various aspects of ministry will train up leaders in all these aspects. People can grow and become equipped and may become ministers themselves because of the excellence of the combination of the ministry gifts together.

The pastor should not be a preacher of doom and gloom. This directly goes against many churches who preach a hell and damnation message regularly. I know it is important that people know about hell and the consequences of rejecting God but I don't believe they should be primary topics every week. The pastor should be an encourager. He or she should use God's word to strengthen and encourager people.

An excellent example of an encouraging pastor is Joel Osteen of Lakewood Church in Houston Texas. It is the largest Church in North America. Of course the people are attracted to the church is because of all of the activities and events and opportunities that I mentioned a large church has but the main reason they go is the pastor brings a word of encouragement every week. He and his wife always bring and encouraging word to the people inspiring them to grab on to God's word as an anchor. The message is to build up and strengthen the sheep. That is why 52, 000 people attend that church. Please know there are many other ministers and many other activities and desirable aspects of the church but being positive for God, and building up faith of the people are the main reasons they gather on a Sunday. Because of the desire for encouragement, millions of people in North America watch the broadcasts of the church services.

The pastor should be aware of the talents and gifts in the church. One thing we had at one of my large churches was a church directory. It had pictures of people (who agreed to be in it) and contact information. We also had a business directory. Because the church was so large, often company owners within our church would be hiring people. The church was a vital connection for those who needed a job and those who had opportunity to hire. Large churches should do our best to care for the congregation. If there is someone who has a need in the church such as financial, we the church should help in some way. If there is a job opportunity, if there is a food pantry etc. These things could make a difference to the members of the church.

A Vision

The pastor and pastoral team should have a vision for the church. There should be a reason they exist. They should have a direction from

God that causes the people to rally. The vision should be clearly visible and communicated to the people regularly through teaching and preaching and aspects of church life. I believe there should be a strong, clear definition of why the church exists. The minimum thing would be that your church exists to care for all the members and so that God would add to the church such as should be saved.

Proverbs 29: 18 Where there is no vision, the people perish;
   but happy is he who keeps the teaching.

I have been to churches that train leaders; I have been to churches that are missionary churches; I have been to churches that are Apostolic and Prophetic. I have been to all sorts of churches that exist for different visions. I believe the pastor and pastoral team should be able to clearly identify the vision of the church. The members should know it and agree with it. It gives direction to the church members. There should be a plan for the church that exceeds one generation. That means you believe that the children you are teaching will grow up and become leaders in the church. You will include them progressively in activity throughout their lives.

Likable people

Pastors should be approachable. That is that someone in the congregation would be able to speak with him or her briefly. I have been to a mega church where the pastor had security guards and no one was able to get to speak with him. Yes, it was a mega church; yes, he was world famous, but if the congregation can never speak with the pastor even for a moment or so, that isn't healthy.

I have been to large congregations, megachurches where the pastor was approachable and humble. The person has got to love people and be a people person or he or she shouldn't be a pastor. I also believe the pastors should not be abused. For instance, I attended a church where the pastors were constantly on call. People called them instead of elders and deacons. People should respect pastors but also be mindful of talking with them – not wasting words. Some pastors are voted in by the congregation or the deacons. Some pastors are appointed. Some inherit the church. Some pastors start a church so they become the pastors. There are different ways for the pastor to be given a sphere of authority. The pastor is accountable to God first and foremost. The pastor does not serve the people; the pastor serves God. The pastor gives and serves among the people but the pastor gives account of his or her sphere of authority to God.

Chapter end questions

1. Consider the pastors that are in your life and explain in what way do you reach you the most: spiritual encouragement, new revelation of God's Word, information or maintenance of the church just as it could be any church.
2. Remember a pastor who influenced you life and explain how it did. Share it with a family member or friend. If you did not pray thanking God for it, do it now. If the person is no longer living, pray for his or her family.
3. Consider a gift or gift certificate or something you could make to give to your pastor that could encourage him or her. Thank God for your pastor.

6 TEACHERS

Teachers

Ephesians 4: 11 He gave some to be apostles, prophets, evangelists, pastors, and teachers, 12 for the equipping of the saints, for the work of service, and for the building up of the body of Christ,

Teachers in the body of Christ, may also be teachers in their career or profession. I have known many such people. I myself am a teacher by profession but also called to teach in the Church. It is not always true, but it is sometimes true that teachers also teach in our school systems. I emphasize this issue because it doesn't necessary have to be true that a teacher in the Church is a teacher in profession. Some with the motivational gift of teaching yearn to contribute in the body of Christ; they should volunteer. Not all people can make a commitment to teach Sunday school; perhaps you could volunteer to teach Vacation Bible School. Also, there are people with a strong desire to teach in the body of Christ who do not have a secular job teaching and may feel unqualified to teach. That is not true either. The desire to do it and the willingness to do it are what you need to get your started.

Desire to Learn

I have known of excellent teachers in the body of Christ who do other professions or who do not have teaching credentials. Secular education is not the factor here but desire to learn and to impart truths are essentials. Teachers are people who desire to learn all they can about God and about the scriptures. Often, they will take notes during a sermon. They will not only take the notes, but often read them over at home. They receive all they can from the preached message. Sometimes these people will study Hebrew or Greek should it be offered as a choice within the local church. I have known of Bible College Professors who know Greek or Hebrew and who are widely renown to congregations for their teaching abilities in the church.

Characteristics of a Teacher

Teachers love God's word. They study it by reading it in context, by comparing it to other scriptures and by reading all instances where it has been mentioned in scripture. Most pastors are teachers by gifting. Teachers don't have to be pastors though. The congregation may have other gifted teachers. Often, they use a concordance and other Bible study books to help them. Sometimes they use commentaries and various versions of the Bible to help them grasp the truths God is revealing. Those motivated by teaching will start volunteering and become known as effective teachers. The Office of teacher is a title one might give to someone has proven the motivational gift of teaching over many years. That person is known for excellence of message, research, anointing and character.

Some modern excellent Bible teachers are Marilyn Hickey, Kenneth and Gloria Copeland, Benny Hinn, Joyce Meyer. Derek Prince was an excellent teacher, as was Myles Monroe. The list can go on and on. These people dedicate themselves to studying God's word, often with several books or Bible helps to get the truths from the scriptures so they can impart them to the people.

My own mother was a teacher but never taught a Bible class, although I am sure she would have liked to do it. She was a teacher by profession (as well as other careers). I would see her studying her Bible, not just reading it. She would sometimes draw things as she read such as the figures that Daniel saw, or that Ezekiel saw. She would sometimes study the maps at the back of the Bible. She wanted all she could get from God's word. It impressed me throughout my life and I would say later once I became a Christian, I developed that same desire to teach God's word and explain it by digging into it myself first.

I would say the scripture's description of the Bereans is a good fit for teachers. They are people who search the scriptures and compare the scriptures. The teacher always sets God's written Word as the standard.

Acts 17: 10 The brothers immediately sent Paul and Silas away by night to Berea. When they arrived, they went into the synagogue of the Jews. 11 These were more noble than those in Thessalonica, for they received the word with all eagerness, daily examining the Scriptures, to find out if these things were so. 12 Therefore many of them believed, including honorable Greek women and many Greek men.

Bible study

The teacher always compares scripture in context with other scripture. The Thompson Chain Reference Bible is an excellent resource for this type of study. Also, the Amplified Bible gives a total literal translation of the scriptures. Years ago, in my early Christian years, there was no Internet. I bought a Bible that had several translations of the New Testament. I delighted in comparing the various versions of the Bible. The teacher often digs and finds what I would call nuggets of gold within the scripture. For instance, the Hebrew or Greek word used actually reveals something profound about the scriptures and when the scriptures are read with that word a new revelation of the scripture is obtained.

2 Timothy 2: 15 Study to show yourself approved by God, a workman who need not be ashamed, rightly dividing the word of truth.

On Line Resources for Teachers

Today, there are so many excellent helps available on the Internet. There are many. I personally use Bible Gateway.com. There is a huge list of translations of the Bible, a concordance and Commentaries. Literally at the click of a button, information can be called, copied and pasted etc. It is an excellent resource that has helped me with me with my own Bible study as well as plan for lessons.

The teacher learns more than he or she teaches

One of the most excellent teachers I had was a successful business man in publishing. He would organize his books and Bibles and spend all afternoon on the Saturday before Sunday school to prepare the word to deliver to our class. His wife informed me he would caution her not to touch any of his books and notes during those precious hours. The truth is he immersed himself in the scriptures in such a way that he could share those truths with us. I often spoke to him about the teachings because they were so excellent. He always admitted that he got more from the studying over of those scriptures and topics than he could possibly convey to us in our class.

Communication Skills

The teaching is a gift. It is of searching for truths in God's word. The person desiring to know truth, should do it; it always compels one to want to share it with others. I know there is a teaching that you may be called as a teacher but may never teach because of your personality and quiet life. I want to share with you that communicating what you have learned can be learned just as one learns how to write a paragraph or how to multiply numbers or how to ride a bike. Communicating truths can and should be taught in our local churches so that people who do not have the secular teaching preparation techniques can be taught to communicate effectively. It could be for one person, for your family, for a small group or to large classes or congregations. Not all teachers are called to teach large congregations but it doesn't make them less effective as a small group teacher or Sunday school teacher.

Perhaps you feel the tugging at your heart as I say the teacher loves to study God's Word and make notes and points based on it. Maybe you feel shy and don't believe you can teach publically. A class in effective oral communications would be excellent for you; an alternative would be purchasing a book or watching videos of effective communication skills. Also, training with a teacher in the body of Christ as an assistant and learning from an experienced teacher can help you to develop as a teacher yourself. I would say knowing the truths God reveals gives you a boldness stronger than any fear or nervousness. You know you have something excellent to share with people that can build them up. It compels you to search the scriptures and to teach.

Desire to discuss Scripture

I gave the example of my mother not teaching a Bible class. It doesn't mean she didn't share. She and I would sometimes (over coffee or a pot of tea) discuss the scriptures and the things she or I had been studying. It was such a precious friendship we had (once we were both Christians) discussing the scriptures and the application of them. A teacher may teach his or her own children or family. A teacher may share things with a friend. My closest friends have been Christians who love to talk about God's word and the conversation that we had about the scriptures are special highlights of our relationship. The teacher has a motivation to share all he or she has studied with the learner who wants to learn.

I thank God for the first Church I attended once I was newly saved. It was known as a teaching church. It was a large church of about 2, 500 people. The pastors were excellent Bible teachers. I took notes every church service. I used to read them over and over during the week. Sometimes I would buy the tape of the sermon so I could listen to it repeatedly throughout the week also. There were at least 20 Bible classes a person could choose to attend before the Sunday service. I took as many different classes as I could as I was driven to learn all that I can to make me an effective Christian. I had such a strong drive in me to learn all I could I took nine-month long Bible studies during the evenings as well as Sunday morning. It sounds radical because it is. I was not the only one. There were about 2, 500 of us who did it. The church had some type of teaching or preaching or ministry almost every day of the week. I want to know all I can. I often made sacrifices of other things as well as finances to get to these classes. I thank God that I did. I do not regret anything I have done to learn more about God.

My testimony about learning to teach

After my first nine-month Bible study to know God and attending Church, my teachers (of the Bible class) asked me to stay on and learn about Spiritual Gifts in the next class they were teaching. I had grown very close to them because of the study of the scriptures with them and was glad to do so. The truths were so strong, because I've shared with you how my teacher studied and researched God's word. After that class was done, the teachers asked me to stay on and help them to teach the Spiritual Gifts class. I wanted to be with them but didn't believe I could do much. I had only been a Christian a little but over a year. First, they gave me tasks such as taking attendance (the class was about 200 people). It made me learn all the people who came to class. I sometimes took special offerings or did tasks that helped the Bible teachers in assistant roles. All the while, I was getting to hear the teaching and receive from the Word of God and I was learning how to put together lessons with scriptures.

Progressive application

At some point during their mentoring of me, they asked me to pray for the class. I was so nervous, I didn't believe I could do it (publicly). They encouraged me and told me to talk to God and focus on it. Afterwards, they used me in other public roles. I joined the nursing home outreach ministry because of them. I would sometimes lead worship or give announcements for our class. I prayed for people to receive the Baptism of the Holy Spirit. All of these things were huge hurdles to me at first because I had no prior knowledge or experience and wasn't raised in a Christian home or in a Christian church. I thank God for Skip and Polly as they poured into me and trained me. They believed in me and made me use gifts and talents that God had given me. I was with them in the Spiritual gifts class several years and not only were the truths engraved into my being but the topic became a passion of mine and I have taught on it to my classes.

Several years later, they started their own church and asked me to teach the youth. I was torn. I loved the church I had attended but also wanted to be with my spiritual parents. I committed myself to my first church Sunday mornings and my spiritual parents church Sunday evenings. They gave me opportunity to preach youth services.

I thank God for them believing in me and teaching me. I believe it is the best way to develop teachers in the church and that is to pair them with experienced teachers and give them opportunity to learn and to apply what they have learned. I didn't know all churches were not like it. It was my first church and God gave me the best possible place. There was so much there to build me up and strengthen me. After several years of taking Bible classes, the strong drive within me to share the word of God became so strong that even though I desired to get in the classes for more teaching, I wanted to sow the word of God into people. I volunteered for Vacation Bible School at more than one church. I started teaching children's Sunday school at my church. It brought such joy to my soul that the words aren't enough to explain the joy I had sharing the things of God with the children.

Your desire to share God's Word with Others

I say this because God may start you learning with passion to learn more, but at some point, the teaching gift within you wants to give not just receive. You may teach one person or share truths with your friends. You may want to start a Sunday school class. God will give you boldness. What literally happens is that you know God has given you so much, you see others who don't have any so you yearn to give to them. It is a spiritual drive within you to want to share what you have learned. I would like to see every church offer Bible classes on other days not just Sundays.

I would like to see other teachers teaching small groups or Bible classes or discipling classes. Those early years of me learning about spiritual gifts has given me a strong drive to see all Christians using their spiritual gifts. I believe their choosing me to be disciple was ordained by God. I have known too many people who have not been given a chance to share what they have learned. It is my desire to see all those with the gift of teaching being utilized in some way within the local church and as an outreach ministry of the Church.

Deacons and Elders

Deacons and Elders within the church should be serving communion, helping the pastor to do visitation and prayer but they often make excellent teachers. They could be teaching small groups or large groups depending on your church. These are proven people who love God and are living a godly life and could invest in people through teaching.

1 Timothy 3: 3 This is a faithful saying: If a man desires the office of an overseer, he desires a good work. 2 An overseer then must be blameless, the husband of one wife, sober, self-controlled, respectable, hospitable, able to teach; 3 not given to drunkenness, not violent, not greedy for money, but

patient, not argumentative, not covetous; 4 and one who manages his own house well, having his children in submission with all reverence.

The teacher in the Body of Christ is held to a high standard. Part of the call to ministry is to live the lifestyle of the kingdom. This has to do with what we do, who we associate with, our character and our fruit. The teacher must live without reproach. The eyes of many will be watching to see if you are truly living your faith. The teacher must first be a mature, devoted, Christian.

Passion for God's word

Teachers do not have to be elders or deacons but they should be mature Christians. New converts could be assistants to mature Christians who could train them to know the way things should be done. What was sown in me by those who cared for my soul and invested in me spiritually has given me a passion for sharing the word of God with others. I've got the desire to train up others because someone invested in me. I realize if no one teaches those who want to be teachers, they may learn bits and pieces of what they receive from television or training, but if someone trains them, they will get the experience from someone who has done it and who is sowing into them so they too might use their gifts and talents. If you treasure God's word for yourself and desire to share it with others, you may have a gifting of teaching. The motivational gift of teaching will get you involved in studying and learning and volunteering and growing

Parables

John 16: 25 "I have told you these things in proverbs. But the time is coming when I will no longer speak to you in proverbs, for I will speak to you plainly about the Father.
Teaching techniques

Jesus used proverbs or as parables as the KJV words it. A good teacher knows how to take a spiritual principle and give examples from everyday life that others can understand to help them understand the new concept. Teachers can take a passage of scripture and break it into teachable units. Part of my studies of becoming an Ontario teacher included the writing of lessons and units of study. A good Bible teacher can do it also. Mostly they learn by experience. It is a matter of pacing the lesson and discussing each part so that all of the lesson is covered.

Proven

Someone gifted by the motivation of teaching will prove himself or herself through a teaching ministry. As with all the ministry gifts, you don't get the title before you have proven yourself by living it out. The evidence of your office of teaching will be in the fruit of your teaching. The teacher will be able to gather people for the purposes of Bible study and others will recognize the gift in him or her. The person's insight and wisdom that comes as he or she is teaching various aspects of scripture becomes so rich and clear that the listeners want more and more of the word.

The person will attract a group of listeners. People will want you to explain the things of God to them. For example, even if the person is not teaching a class, the person may be speaking with someone and he or she may ask questions that the teacher can answer. It is more than simply a friendly chat. The teacher brings scripture, insight, wisdom and application with his or her words. His or her words are meaningful. People know them to be experts on certain topics.

Structure

The person motivated by teaching must learn simple things such as organization of material. Most 40 min – 1 hour minute Bible classes should have a minimum of 3 main points. Each main point should have scriptures, details, examples and information to help the class comprehend the lesson. Textbooks are written that way; experienced teachers use the same type of pattern. Most packaged Church curriculum uses the same formula. A new teacher should be taught simple things such as these. The best way to learn is by being with experienced teachers who can teach by showing and giving opportunities to the new recruits.

Topics

The new teacher should teach on topics he or she is knowledgeable in. It could be a book or Bible study that is purchased. It could be existing Church curriculum. Almost always, there should be more than enough information for the teacher so that he or she can choose what to use during the delivery of the message. Topics for Bible studies are limitless. There could be Bible classes such as I first took that are introductions to the doctrines, covenants, sacraments etc. There could be Bible classes on prayer, on worship and praise, on stewardship. The Bible is more than simply a history book. It is a life application book to help us live our lives. Scripture convers all aspects of human life. We should offer a variety of classes to the congregation so that all different types of people are being strengthened and built up.

A Teacher uses the Old Testament and The New Testament

There should be teachings from the Old Testament as well as the New Testament. Both are important and both apply to our lives. Often scriptures from the Old testament are spoken of or quoted by the writers of the New Testament. There should be classes on topics from the Old Testament and New Testament. Most of my Bible teachers would use a variety of scriptures from both.

Diversity of course offerings means more people can be built up; more people will be attracted. For example, there could be Christian exercise classes who use scripture ad praise and worship to help them be motivated. There could be teaching on stewardship and finances; there could be teaching on the prophetic; there could be teaching on the Jewish festivals that God established or the Book of Hebrews. There could be a historical study of a prophet's life. The list of possible topics is infinite because the Bible is a Divinely inspired Book. It is not possible for a pastor to do all of this along with his or her other duties, that is why we should be releasing teachers into their giftings and training them to teach so that they too will be able to teach Bible classes training others.

It is a principle used throughout the Bible of an elder training the youths. Usually, one generation older is best to teach an age group 1 generation below it. There are exceptions to this of course. For instance, I enjoy teaching children and do it to keep children as a part of my life. I am much older than the children, but as teaching them, but I always learn something about them while I am doing it. Keeping people of all different ages in my life helps me to be a more effective Christian communicator and intercessor.

Should you find an Excellent Teacher

If you find a class taught by an excellent teacher, take other courses with him or her. I believe that the teacher not only teaches the subject matter but also makes an impartation into the person's life. Often there are social functions in the class and gatherings. There are mature Christians; press into them and learn all you can from them. It is a type of discipling. You have got to want to learn and grown spiritually to do it. Consider meeting with the experienced teacher for a coffee to discuss your desire to teach. Plan several questions you would ask of how to be excellent.

Teachers are Learners first

Every semester (teachers think in semesters more than in seasons) since I got saved, I have taken some type of Bible study as it was offered as long as I attended those churches that offered them. As soon as I got the Internet, I began listening and watching excellent preaching and teaching. I have invested in my spiritual growth as a priority; I was the first Christian in my family. Later my mother received the LORD. I do not regret one penny I have spent on hundreds of tapes, CDS DVDs and books. These have been my main teachers in recent years. Because of my current Church situation, I rely on Christian Internet and resources such as magazines, books etc. to help me learn. I want to keep learning about God all my life. I believe that in the life to come, I will spend all eternity learning about God. I believe that a good teacher must also want to keep learning. The day a teacher stops learning new things, he or she becomes less effective in his or her gifting.

Christian Satellite

I don't know what type of church you go to but if you do not have the variety of teaching topics I have mentioned, Christian television is an excellent support. Glory Star is a Christian Satellite system where you can get about 70 stations of Christian broadcasting. It includes teaching and preaching, entertainment, Christian and family type movies, documentaries etc. The cost covers the satellite receiver and dish. I mention it because I had this system and it was such a blessing to me. I could get the best types of Christian preaching from Apostles, Prophets, Pastors, Teachers, Evangelists etc. All of the programming is free. There is no monthly fee. I am sure there are other Christians who desire extra teaching of God's word who would find it as an excellent resource. You must use discernment. Not everyone on the television or cable network is a true teacher or preacher. Even if there is excellent teaching and preaching, you are not going to feel a connection with all of the ministers. I thank God for Christian Media because it has been an important part of my life since I was newly saved. Often the only Christian I saw during my week was the people at Church and those on Christian media.

Closing Comments

If you desire to teach or feel a motivation to share God's word, pray for God to give you the right connections and to direct your steps. If the teaching of this chapter has tugged at your heart in any way with a desire to teach or to disciple someone, please try approaching your pastor with the idea. I believe pastors would welcome something that would be good for the sheep. The pastor must know you are a Christian and you must be known to be a mature Christian; these are prerequisites for ministry.

If you want to teach but are a new Christian, volunteer to help a teacher with his or her class. You could do photocopying or run an electronic projector etc. You could be learning from someone so that soon you too could be entrusted to teach a class. A wise pastor will welcome new course offerings of new classes and new opportunities for others to learn, including newer Christians to be trained to be a teacher. Pray about your desire to teach others. Volunteer to help or to start a class. Don't let the gift be dormant. It is given to you so that you might develop it and use it for God's glory and the building up of the Church.

Chapter end questions

1. If you teach a Bible class in your church explain why you do it. If you do not, explain why you do not.
2. Consider any Bible teachers who taught you the word of God wither in person or on TV. Pray for them or their families thanking God for the gift.
3. Name 2- 3 Bible teachers from media who have influenced your life. Try to remember specifically what you learned from them.
4. If you have a desire to share God's word consider helping with Vacation Bible school, Sunday school or some other teaching volunteer position. Perhaps you could invite some friends to your home for a Bible study.

7 CONCLUSION

Ministry gifts

Manifestational gifts are given to each person in the Body of Christ and it possible for God to use any Christian in any of them: tongues, interpretation of tongues, prophecy, word of wisdom, word of knowledge, discerning of spirits, gift of faith, gift of working of miracles, gifts of healing. They are developed by using them. It is possible to learn your motivational gifts and how to use them in the church: giving, serving, leadership, exhortation, mercy, prophecy, and teaching

Ministry gifts are special invitations from God and should you be called into ministry God will tug at your heart and direct you so you can function in the five-fold ministry – the Hand of Christ in the earth: apostles, prophets, evangelists, pastors and teachers. The ministry gifts are God's gifts to the Church.

Ephesians 4: 11 He gave some to be apostles, prophets, evangelists, pastors, and teachers, 12 for the equipping of the saints, for the work of service, and for the building up of the body of Christ, 13 until we all come into the unity of the faith and of the knowledge of the Son of God, into a complete man, to the measure of the stature of the fullness of Christ, 14 so we may no longer be children, tossed here and there by waves and carried about with every wind of doctrine by the trickery of men, by craftiness with deceitful scheming. 15 But, speaking the truth in love, we may grow up in all things into Him, who is the head, Christ Himself, 16 from whom the whole body is joined together and connected by every joint and ligament, as every part effectively does its work and grows, building itself up in love.

The ministry gifts are given to the Church vs 13 until we all come into the unity of the faith and of the knowledge of the Son of God, into a complete man, to the measure of the stature of the fullness of Christ,

The ministry gifts are to build up, strengthen and cause the Church to be complete resembling Christ in the earth. Also, so that we might grown in Christ building up and strengthening the other parts of the Body of Christ around us.

If only the Apostle were needed, God would have given us plenty of Apostles, but he also gave us prophets, evangelists, pastors and teachers. He gave them to us because for the Church to be built up and complete, all of those ministry gifts need to function in the body. The only person who ever had all the ministry gifts was Jesus Himself. I do believe that we can use a ministry gift in proper alignment with other ministry gifts so that we move together as a hand that grasps and object such as a ball and can throw it. It requires total agreement of all the fingers and muscles connected to be able to do it. Should God give you opportunity to learn from a mature minister of the gospel as an apprentice would learn from a master craftsman, you should prayerfully consider it. Those opportunities are not usually plentiful but they are life changing.

If you feel a desire in your heart towards any of the ministry gifts, do your part to learn all you can about them. Take Bible classes that teach on them. If you know someone at your church who has a certain ministry gift you feel a calling towards, take classes with him or her. You could invite the person to lunch or dinner and treat him or her. Prepare questions you have about ministry for your discussion. Listen to what they are saying knowing it can help you.

Get Christian Media and search for those who have the ministry gift you feel the calling towards. Watch them. Take notes. Try to observe how the gospel is shared through them as well as the message they bring. I mean the delivery of the message. For example, the number of main points in the sermon; the use of objects or visuals or illustrated sermons, body posture, voice tone, altar call. Notice all aspects of the ministry.

Should there be no person in your local church with the ministry gift you feel drawn to, do all you can to get a chance to speak with the TV minister. Keep it brief. Keep it focused on what you can learn. Perhaps the person teaches Bible courses etc. Don't go outside the parameters of your purpose. Your purpose to learn all you can from someone with a ministry gift you feel called to. Invest in yourself books, CD's DVD's, conferences, an on line Bible course etc. Perhaps you will know that you should go to Bible College.

Keep teachable. Keep humble. Get connected with people of like precious faith who have the same giftings. Keep your mouth speaking in alignment with God's Word. Pray seeking God specifically about the ministry gift and ask God to reveal to you what to do, where you should be, how you can develop your giftings while learning and while building up the Body of Christ. Ministry gifts are a sharing of the labour with Jesus Christ Himself. He served and gave and lived His life so that we might know Him. It is essential that ministers of the gospel live their lives wholly for Jesus. It is important to be with a Shepherd or pastor who knows your gifts and who will follow the promptings of the Holy Spirit. Consecrate yourself, if you haven't already done so. Give yourself, your education, your experience, your spirit, your soul, your body to God wholly. Pray that He will lead you and direct you to places of learning and training.

Romans 12: 1 I urge you therefore, brothers, by the mercies of God, that you present your bodies as a living sacrifice, holy, and acceptable to God, which is your reasonable service of worship. 2 Do not be conformed to this world, but be transformed by the renewing of your mind, that you may prove what is the good and acceptable and perfect will of God.

1 Thessalonians 5: 23 May the very God of peace sanctify you completely. And I pray to God that your whole spirit, soul, and body be preserved blameless unto the coming of our Lord Jesus Christ.

Those the most important things you can do once you feel a tug at your heart for ministry. Pray Believing God will use you, train you, bless you.
I pray this book has given you information, insight, and instruction on pursuing the different ministry gifts and in knowing how they function. Any of the preachers or teachers mentioned in this book are excellent resources for you to go to their websites and learn from their ministries.

PRAYERS

Prayer of Consecration

God I give myself to you, spirit, soul and body. I want what you want for my life. Align me with the Word of God. Align me with people of like precious faith. Connect me with people who can teach me and direct me. Let me use all my gifts and talents for you. In Jesus Name, Amen.

Prayer of Salvation

Jesus, I believe you died for my sins and purchased my life so that I may be free from sin, hell and the garve. I want to know you. Forgive me for my sins. Wash me in your blood. Fill me with your Holy Spirit. Give me boldness about Christ. Help me to read and understand the Bible. Lead me to people who can encourage me in being a Christian and living for you. Help me to find a Christian Church where they believe the Word of God and the gifts of the Spirit. Amen.

Prayer for Baptism of the Holy Spirit.

Jesus I thank you for drawing me. Holy Spirit I thank you that you live inside of me. You promised that we would be filled with the Holy Spirit and baptized in the Holy Spirit. I want your best for me. I want to be filled with the Holy Spirit to overflowing. I seek you for it. I believe you will give me what I've asked for because it is your promise. O Jesus I thank you…(begin to thank Him for things He has done for you). O Jesus I praise you…(Begin to praise him for things He has done and how good He has been to you.) O Jesus I worship you…(begin to thank Him for His beauty and the peace that He brings and the overwhelming love of His presence. As you worship say the words "I worship you" and let them come from your innermost being. It is not a magic formula. It is a way of getting you to think of God more than anything else. Focus on Him and expect He will fill you and baptize you in the Holy Spirit. As words in other languages come to you say them.   Let the praise s and worship roll from out of your innermost being.

It will bubble up like a fountain. Give yourself wholly as you worship. Give yourself room so you're not just squeezing it in.

Prayer for stirring up the gifts

Literally pray over yourself for at least 30 minutes.
I stir the gift of faith. I stir the gifts of the working of miracles. I stir the. gifts of healing. I stir the gift of word of wisdom. I stir the gift of word of knowledge. I stir the gift of discerning of spirits. I stir the gift of tongues. I stir the gift of interpretation of tongues. I stir the gift of prophecy.
God use me in the gifts of the Spirit. Quicken me in the gifts of the Spirit so I might be used by you today.
Also pray

I stir the gift of encouragement. I stir the gift of giving. I stir the gift of serving. I stir the gift of teaching. I stir the gift of leadership.

Prayer over youself for Godly Character. Go to

Galatians 5: 22 But the fruit of the Spirit is love, joy, peace, patience, gentleness, goodness, faith, 23 meekness, and self-control; against such there is no law. 24 Those who are Christ's have crucified the flesh with its passions and lusts. 25 If we live in the Spirit, let us also walk in the Spirit.

Don't just read the word; pray it. God I desire the fruits of love. I want the fruit of peace and patience. God make me gentle and good. I want the fruit of faith. Let me be meek and humble with excellence and integrity. Let me be temperate. Let me know your leading and guiding in all areas of my life. I desire Godly character in me. Transform me O God. Amen.

Prayer for a mentor

O God, you have placed within my heart a desire to minister in….. (name the ministry gift) God lead me to people who can help me develop this gift so that I can function in it for your glory. Give me divine connections. Bring people to my memory or into my life that I can contact who can help me develop my gifts for your glory. I say yes to you God. Lead me Holy Spirit. Amen.

OTHER BOOKS BY CHRIS LEGEBOW

Available on Amazon.ca Amazon.com or Amazon.ca or Kindle
Or the Create Space webstore.

Living Word Publishers

An Excellent Spirit: Living Life Wholly Unto God

Covenant With God: God's Relationship With Man

Discovering and Using your Spiritual Gifts

The Five-Fold Ministry: Gifts to the Church

Kinds of Prayer. Knowing Them and Using Them Effectively

Living Life Fully: Knowing your Purpose

The Anointing: the Glory of God

The High Calling: Life Worth Living

The Sacraments: A Charismatic Guide

ABOUT THE AUTHOR

ABOUT THE AUTHOR

Chris Legebow is a Christian Professor of English and Communications. She has taught at the elementary, high school and College and University levels. She has ministered in her local churches in intercessory prayer, teaching Sunday school and other Christian Doctrine classes to children and youths. She has preached to congregations and given her testimony. Although she was not raised in a Christian home, she came to know Jesus Christ as her Saviour and LORD while she was studying in University. This radically transformed her life in terms of priorities and commitment. She has a strong passion for the great commission – that Jesus Christ would be preached throughout all the earth believing that it a major sign of the LORD's return. She has been a part of several different types of full gospel charismatic churches but has also gained much of her insight and enlightenment from Christian Media and broadcasting. She hopes to continue ministering, serving, interceding and giving and teaching until the LORD returns.

www.ingramcontent.com/pod-product-compliance
Lightning Source LLC
Chambersburg PA
CBHW020512030426
42337CB00011B/350